Writing with Style

Series Editor: DR REBECCA STOTT

SPEAK
WRITE
SERIES

Other titles in the series:

Grammar and Writing
Rebecca Stott and Peter Chapman (Eds)

Speaking your Mind: Oral Presentation and Seminar Skills
Rebecca Stott, Tory Young and Cordelia Bryan (Eds)

Making your Case: A Practical Guide to Essay Writing
Rebecca Stott, Anna Snaith and Rick Rylance (Eds)

Writing with Style

Edited by Rebecca Stott and Simon Avery

Series Editor: Rebecca Stott

An imprint of **Pearson Education**

Harlow, England · London · New York · Reading, Massachusetts · San Francisco · Toronto · Don Mills, Ontario · Sydney
Tokyo · Singapore · Hong Kong · Seoul · Taipei · Cape Town · Madrid · Mexico City · Amsterdam · Munich · Paris · Milan

England

and Associated Companies throughout the world

Visit us on the World Wide Web at:
http://www.pearsoneduc.com

First published 2001

This edition © Pearson Education Limited 2001
Introduction and Chapters 1 and 4 © Rebecca Stott 2001
Chapter 2 © Anna Snaith 2001
Chapter 3 © Simon Avery 2001
Chapter 5 © Simon Featherstone 2001
Chapter 6 © Dominic Rowland and Simon Avery 2001

ISBN 0 582 38242 4

British Library Cataloguing-in-Publication Data
A catalogue record for this book is available from the British Library

Library of Congress Cataloging-in-Publication Data
Writing with style / edited by Rebecca Stott and Simon Avery.
     p. cm. — (Speak-write series)
     Includes index.
     ISBN 0-582-38242-4 (pbk.)
     1. English language—Rhetoric. 2. English language—Style. 3. Journalism—
Authorship. 4. Report writing. I. Stott, Rebecca. II. Avery, Simon. III. Series.

PE1408.W776 2000   00-032123

10 9 8 7 6 5 4 3 2 1
04 03 02 01

Typeset by 35 in 10.5/12.5 Janson
Printed and bound in Malaysia, LSP

CONTENTS

AUTHOR'S
ACKNOWLEDGEMENTS

This book and the other three books in the Speak–Write Series, *Grammar and Writing, Making your Case: A Practical Guide to Essay Writing* and *Speaking your Mind: Oral Presentation and Seminar Skills*, have been three years in the making. They are the result of three years of research, teaching design and piloting undertaken by the Speak–Write Project, established by the English Department of Anglia Polytechnic University in Cambridge and funded by the Higher Education Funding Council for England through its Fund for the Development of Teaching and Learning. The Speak–Write Project was set up to respond to claims from members of English departments across the country that first-year undergraduates needed more intensive advanced writing and speaking courses at foundation level in order to perform more effectively in higher education.

Although the Speak–Write Project looked closely at freshman rhetoric and composition classes which have run successfully in the United States for decades, the Speak–Write designers and researchers concluded that there was a need in British higher education for innovative communication skills courses which were embedded in specific subject areas and not generic skills courses alone. These four books have been piloted, designed and adapted by and for lecturers and students working in English literature departments and much of the material presented for analysis or rewriting or adaptation is of a literary kind. This said, the books have a much wider application and can be adapted for use by a range of cognate disciplines in the Humanities.

The Speak–Write books have drawn on the imaginations, time and work of many people. The editors and authors of individual books and chapters are acknowledged beneath the chapter and book titles. Many more people and institutions have contributed who remain invisible and I would like to thank as many of them individually here as possible: Tory Young, Editorial

Assistant, who saw the books through their final metamorphosis, tirelessly and with great good humour and editorial skill; Ruth Maitland, the Speak–Write Project's Administrator, who held everything together; Rob Pope (Oxford Brookes University), Stephen Minta (York University), Val Purton (City College, Norwich), Morag Styles (Homerton College, Cambridge) and Katy Wales (Leeds University), the External Readers who assessed and advised on early drafts of the books; Paul Boyd, Richard James, Regine Hasseler, Shelby Bohland and Lucy Wood, the student editorial advisory group; Elizabeth Mann, Commissioning Editor at Longman, for her encouragement and enthusiasm for the Project in its early stages; staff and students of the English Department at Anglia Polytechnic University who have refined and shaped the books through giving continual feedback on aspects of teaching and learning; and my first-year students of 1999 in particular for applying their creative minds to difficult editorial decisions.

Rebecca Stott, *Series Editor*

PUBLISHER'S ACKNOWLEDGEMENTS

We are grateful to the following for permission to reproduce copyright material:

2000, Apple Computer, Inc. for an extract from an iMac® advertisement "Apple, the Apple logo, FireWire® and iMac TM® are registered trademarks. Apple Computer, Inc. registered in the United States and other countries" FireWire® and iMac TM® are Trademarks of Apple Computer Inc; European Magazines Ltd for the text from the review of 'Grease' in *MARIE CLAIRE* July 1998; Guardian Newspapers Ltd for extract from the article 'Asylum seekers free to stay' by Alan Travis in *THE GUARDIAN* 28.7.98; The writer, Michael Jarman for the letter on page 98; Plain English Campaign for an extract from *THE PLAIN ENGLISH STORY*; Premier Brands UK Ltd/Cadbury Schweppes for the advertising slogan 'Hot chocolate drinking chocolate'; Taylor & Francis for an adapted table 'Analysing in Detail' from *THE ENGLISH STUDIES BOOK* by Rob Pope, published by Routledge; Universal Music Publishing Limited/Dick James Music Limited for the lyrics from the song 'Love is all around' (Presley) © 1967; The Victoria and Albert Museum for the Charles Dickens 'Bleak House' draft image; Windswept Music London for the lyrics from the song 'A case of you' written by Joni Mitchell first published by Joni Mitchell Publishing © 1971 by Joni Mitchell/BMI; Woolworths plc for the slogan 'That's the Wonder of Woolworth'.

We have been unable to trace the copyright holders of 'New Improved Sonnet XVIII' by Peter Titheradge and would appreciate any information which would enable us to do so.

INTRODUCTION

Rebecca Stott

Like stones, words are laborious and unforgiving, and the fitting of them together, like the fitting of stones, demands great patience and strength of purpose and particular skill.

(Edmund Morrison)

Writing is the hardest way of earning a living, with the possible exception of wrestling alligators.

(Olin Miller)

Writing is a craft – and a difficult one. Whether a writer is writing a novel or a set of instructions for assembling a futon, the words s/he chooses to assemble into sentences will have to be drafted and drafted again. Writing of whatever kind is not just about having something to say (although you cannot begin with nothing to say), it is also about struggling with the words on paper. Patience, strength of purpose, deliberation and skill are all essential qualities of a writer working to perfect his or her craft.

When we read a piece of published prose, of course, we see nothing of this struggle with words. Everything we see is likely to be smooth and fluent and polished. It is easy to forget that the text has a history; the manuscript (sometimes there will be several) of a text gives us the record of that history. When we do get to see a hand-written manuscript, with its crossings-out and substituted words, we are peeking behind the scenes – at the work in progress. Look at the differences between the published opening of Chapter 11 of Dickens's *Bleak House* (1853), for instance, and the manuscript version of that same paragraph. Here is the published version:

A touch on the lawyer's wrinkled hand as he stands in the dark room, irresolute, makes him start and say, 'What's that?'

'It's me,' returns the old man of the house, whose breath is in his ear. 'Can't you wake him?'

'No.'

'What have you done with your candle?'

'It's gone out. Here it is.'

Krook takes it, goes to the fire, stoops over the red embers, and tries to get a light. The dying ashes have no light to spare, and his endeavours are vain. Muttering, after an ineffectual call to his lodger, that he will go downstairs and bring a lighted candle from the shop, the old man departs. Mr. Tulkinghorn, for some new reason that he has, does not await his return in the room, but on the stairs outside.

(Dickens 1977: 125)

And here is the manuscript version showing Dickens's original workings:

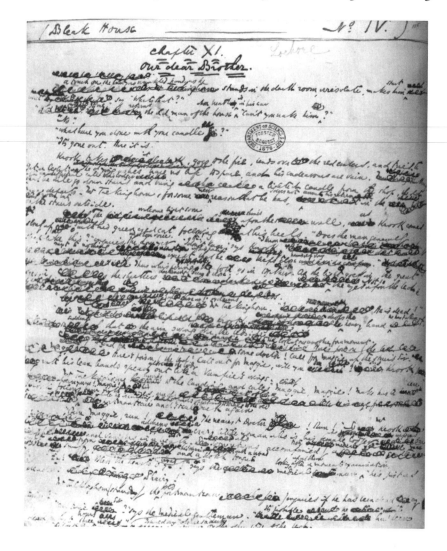

Drafting and redrafting is the daily business of the writer and this book will have a good deal to say about the practicalities of writing in general and drafting in particular. Although many of the earliest manuscripts of famous novels are safely tucked away in archives in libraries all over the world, literary scholars tend to consult them only if they are preparing editions of the text (to check a newly published edition against an earlier version, for instance) or if they are studying the prose style of the author. As a result, lecturers, literary critics and literature students work mostly with finished texts. However, a close look at manuscript versions can give us valuable information about the stages of a writer's craft and the extent of the writer's revisions. Many writers also write very astutely about the writing process, often in the form of letters to other writers or essays written for young writers.

These days, of course, many writers do not produce hand-written manuscripts but instead work with word-processors. This does not mean that the drafting is any less important. The process of writing with a word-processor is just different and in some ways easier, although it opens up different kinds of problems for some writers. After all, 'cut and paste' is something achieved in a second with a word-processor, but once that paragraph has been moved to a new place in the text, its original position becomes untraceable, except with certain kinds of software, and sometimes the writer needs to be able to retrace earlier decisions and changes. This book, for instance, written on several different computers by the authors of individual chapters and e-mailed to the editor, assembled into one document, edited, copy-edited and finally proof-read, has gone through many, many drafts over a three-year period. Some chapters have been drafted more than others, depending on the problems faced by the editors and authors and on the material in the chapters. However, none of our editorial and authorial decisions and problems and struggles is visible to you now. The work needed to produce this book has involved numerous people: publishers, external readers, students asked to comment on individual chapters, authors and editors. Writing is rarely a completely isolated activity. Even novelists and poets depend upon other people reading and commenting on their work and editors helping to make decisions about the final shape of the book. Very little writing is done by one person in complete isolation and in this book we have made group work an essential part of the writing and drafting process.

This book is about style and craft in prose writing and about the many practical, small-scale changes that a writer can make to a text in order to achieve certain effects in his or her prose style. We wanted to write a book which would put together some general principles for effective prose writing, principles that would be relevant to all kinds of writers producing all kinds of prose writing (from business writing to creative writing, for instance). We found that, of the many books published on language and writing skills, most were either books on stylistics (the study of prose style in literary studies) or general books of advice on how to write more effectively. We have tried to write a book which combines these two kinds of books since we believe that effective writing is achieved in part through practice and in part through becoming more aware of what makes writing effective by reading and analysing texts by established writers.

This book will therefore introduce you to stylistic analysis and to the principles of advanced writing. It works, as we have said, from the position that language is a craft that can be mastered with practice, that advanced writing skills are best learned from those who are already effective writers, and that any judgement about the quality of writing must take into account the use to which it is put and the audience for whom it is intended. Highly poetic and literary prose would probably become ineffective writing if it were used in an instruction manual, for instance.

How to use this book

The writing in this book will be drawn from a range of different contexts, cultures and historical periods. It will include business English, letters, journalism, comedy writing and instruction manuals, as well as the prose of literary texts. The activities in the book are designed to develop your writing and analytical skills in a variety of ways. Sometimes we will ask you to analyse a certain piece of prose; sometimes we will ask you to rewrite or imitate it or adapt it for different purposes. The activities in each chapter have different levels of difficulty and some will take much longer than others. Whether you are working through this book alone or in the company of others in a seminar or tutorial, you will gain the maximum benefit from this book by undertaking every activity in each chapter. However, you might want to concentrate more on stylistic analysis or on writing – in which case you might only choose a selection of activities. The final chapter, 'Styles of journalism', has been designed to consolidate much of the material introduced in earlier chapters and contains more activities.

Reference

Dickens, Charles (1977) *Bleak House: An Authoritative and Annotated Text* [1853]. New York: W.W. Norton & Company.

Style in writing

Rebecca Stott

What is style?

Style is the word we use to describe *how* speakers or writers say whatever it is they say. It is their *manner* of expression in language. Traditionally, the study of style has been developed in literary criticism and so it is particularly associated with literary texts. However, in its broadest sense style can be applied to spoken and written, literary and non-literary varieties of language. A literary critic might study the style used in a particular text or the style of a particular author or the style of a particular period of literary history, such as the Victorian novel for instance. A literary critic concerned with stylistics is likely to be interested in:

- the choice of words (diction)
- the sentence structure and word order
- the use of figurative language (metaphors and similes)
- the use of patterns of rhythm and sound
- the use of rhetorical aims and devices.

Often a prose style is said to be like a signature or a fingerprint. When an art expert is given an unsigned picture to identify as a Van Gogh or a Rembrandt, he or she looks at the way the paint is laid on the canvas, the type of paint used, the method of building up the picture, the mixture of brush-strokes used and so on. He or she would be looking to identify the distinctive *style* of Van Gogh or Rembrandt, something that is unique to that particular painter. The art critic would also be well-informed about particular changes in the artist's style of painting. Picasso, for instance, went through many different 'periods' in which his style changed dramatically.

It is similar with writing. Each writer develops his or her own distinctive style and quite often we do not need to be an expert to recognise the author of a particular piece of writing, if we know his or her work well. A parody (a comic imitation of a piece of writing) relies on people recognising a particular style which is being mimicked.

However, very few writers have a prose style that does not change. Usually writers develop their styles and techniques through time; the prose style of Dickens's early writing is different from his late writing, because he found new ways of working and new ways of crafting sentences, just as Michelangelo changed the way he sculpted blocks of marble, learning new techniques all the time. Henry James's change in style is a famous example. Some critics claim that there is a distinct point in James's writing where his style changes and becomes even more convoluted. This, they claim, is the point at which James began to dictate his novels to a secretary working on a typewriter. As a result of dictating his story, his sentences changed shape, became longer and more heavily subordinated.

Sentence structure is an important consideration in the study of style, but it is only one of a number of factors which need to be taken into account. It would be ridiculous to assume, for instance, that novelists tend to use only one dominant kind of sentence structure, just as it would be ridiculous to assume that a painter only uses one kind of brush-stroke. It is a particular *combination* of characteristics that make up what we call a prose style. For instance, in an essay published in 1970 Louis T. Milic argued that the prose style of the seventeenth-century writer Jonathan Swift was not characterised solely by his liking for particular kinds of sentence structures, but by his heavy use of connectives ('and', 'but', 'for', 'however') in particular. Milic argued that Swift used all these connectives to move the reader swiftly through the line of his arguments. In a detailed study Milic found that Swift started one sentence in every five with a coordinating conjunction and one in three with a connective of some sort (Milic 1970: 246).

Prose styles can be described in many different ways using words such as ornate, pure, simple, rhetorical, elaborate, flamboyant, discursive, baroque and so on. Styles can also be classified according to a type of writing (genre), so a prose style might be described as 'scientific' or 'journalistic' or 'legalistic'. If the prose style is considered to be like that of another writer it might be described as 'Miltonic' or 'Shakespearean' or 'Keatsian'. Sometimes prose styles are easily recognisable as typical of a particular historical period. In the seventeenth and eighteenth centuries, for instance, writers interested in language distinguished between a vogue for writing in the 'Ciceronian style' (influenced by the Roman writer Cicero) and a vogue for writing in the Senecan style (influenced by the Roman writer Seneca). The first style used complex sentences, building to a climax, keeping the main verb right to the end of the sentence (what is called a periodic sentence). The second was much more clipped, concise and epigrammatic. This shows how complex the evolution of prose style is. When a certain writer is in vogue, his or her prose style will influence the next generation, who will adapt it and make it their own.

Virginia Woolf in her fantasy-biography *Orlando* (1928) creates something of a light-hearted history of English prose style. Throughout the novel the hero/heroine (the character changes sex in the middle of the novel) is trying to write a long poem called 'The Oak Tree'. As Orlando lives through several hundred years without dying or even ageing, each time s/he tries to write a section of the poem s/he finds herself affected by the style of writing of that particular period of history. Woolf is suggesting that the *way* people write has something to do with the world in which they live. When Orlando tries to write in the early Victorian period, for instance, s/he finds that all her sentences are very long and elaborate, and the biographer comments on this:

> for there is no stopping damp; it gets into the inkpot as it gets into the woodwork – sentences swelled, adjectives multiplied, lyrics became epics, and little trifles that had been essays a column long were now encyclopaedias in ten or twenty volumes.

> (Woolf 1963: 162)

ACTIVITY 1:

Collect examples of a variety of styles of writing from newspapers, magazines, novels, plays, textbooks and any other kinds of document. Attempt to categorise them as genres and to characterise their differences in terms of word choice, sentence structures, layout and so on.

Fitting style to a purpose

Prose styles develop through time, just as people do, since language is an organism which adapts and grows with the people who use it. New styles come into use because writers need a variety of different styles to write texts for different audiences. Developments in materials, media and technology also inspire new styles: think for instance of the styles and genres of radio DJs, cartoons, e-mail messages and internet sites.

This book, however, does not aim only to develop the ability to analyse texts and their prose styles. It is also a book about practical writing skills. Therefore where we do analyse the style of a particular writer or of a particular text it will help us understand some general principles behind effective writing. We will not be looking only at the styles of literary writers either, but also at those of writers working in different contexts and for different audiences: writing for business, journalism and advertising, for instance. As we said in the Introduction, this book begins with the principle that the craft of writing is best understood through both analysis and practice. All crafts are learned to some extent by a combination of hard work and discipline and the study of those who have already mastered the particular skill, whether these are sculptors, web-designers or writers.

The nineteenth-century novelist George Eliot was one of many writers constantly on the look-out for new writing techniques, reading books of all kinds. Here she is writing to a friend in 1861 about her struggle to find a style for *The Mill on the Floss* which was somewhere between formal and colloquial. In her search she did not stay sitting at her desk, trying to work it out, but instead she wandered around her library, picking up books by writers she liked who had already found a way of achieving what she wanted to do:

> It seems to me that I have discerned such shades very strikingly rendered in Balzac, and occasionally in George Sand. Balzac, I think, dares to be thoroughly colloquial, in spite of French strait-lacing. Even in English this daring is far from being general. The writers who dare to be thoroughly familiar are Shakespeare, Fielding, Scott (where he is expressing the popular life with which he is familiar), and indeed every other writer of fiction of the first class. Even in his loftiest tragedies – in Hamlet, for example – Shakespeare is intensely colloquial. One hears the very accent of living men.

> (George Eliot, Letter to Francois D'Albert Durade,
> 29 January 1861, quoted in Allott 1973: 314)

A more modern writer and poet, Seamus Heaney, once claimed in an essay called 'Feeling into Words' that it was only through reading that he found his way to writing, because in reading certain writers he gradually found a rhythm that felt familiar to him, a style that he could make his own. He described this process as tuning his 'own proper music' to the sounds and rhythms which moved him in his reading:

> How, then, do you find it? In practice, you hear it coming from some-body else, you hear something in another writer's sounds that flows in through your ear and enters the echo-chamber of your head and delights your whole nervous system in such a way that your reaction will be, 'Ah, I wish I had said that, in that particular way.' This other writer, in fact, has spoken something essential to you, something you recognise instinct-ively as a true sounding of aspects of yourself and your experience. And your first steps as a writer will be to imitate, consciously or unconsciously, those sounds that flowed in, that in-fluence.

> (Heaney 1980: 44–5)

Heaney is describing in this passage his reaction to a style of writing which is in tune with his 'own music'; in *A Room of One's Own* (1929) Virginia Woolf describes reacting to a style of writing which is out of tune with hers. Here she describes picking up a novel by Mary Carmichael called *Life's Adventure* and reading the first page:

> To begin with, I ran my eye up and down the page. I am going to get the hang of her sentences first, I said, before I load my memory with blue eyes and brown and the relationship that there may be between Chloe and Roger. There will be time for that when I have decided whether she has a pen in her hand or a pickaxe. So I tried a sentence or two on my tongue. Soon it was obvious that something was not quite in order. The smooth gliding of sentence after sentence was interrupted. Something tore, some-thing scratched; a single word here and there flashed its torch into my eyes. . . . Alas, I sighed, that it should be so. For while Jane Austen breaks from melody to melody as Mozart from song to song, to read this writing was like being out at sea in an open boat. Up one went, down one sank.
>
> (Woolf 1929: 120–21)

However, although Woolf finds Carmichael an 'awkward writer' with a 'terse' and 'shortwinded' prose style, there is much in the rest of the novel she admires. She finds, for instance, that Carmichael has 'a sensibility that was very wide, eager and free' and this makes her prepared to overlook many of the faults in the writing. What is interesting, though, is the way Woolf describes the effect of the prose style not just as sound and melody but as a series of physical sensations that a reader feels: such as going up and down in a boat, being scratched, and even having a flashlight shone in one's face. The sentences seem to have a life of their own.

ACTIVITY 2:

Identify a writer whose style you find in some way interesting or irritating. Concentrate on a few passages and try to say what is distinctive about her or his style. Go on to attempt a few lines imitating or parodying that style, perhaps through treating a different topic in a similar way.

Writing about prose style

When literary critics and students of literature study prose style in a sustained way, attempting to discover what it is that is unique about a particular writer or characteristics of a period or type of writing, they must, of course, look at a passage or series of passages in detail. They are likely to be looking for information about the author's word choice, word combination, use of patterns of sound and rhythm, favoured types of sentence construction and so on. They will also be concerned with how these features contribute to the overall effect of the piece. It is important when analysing a piece of prose to balance the questions about the linguistic features with considerations about the effect of the piece. A list of observations of linguistic features alone is likely to be dull and a little pointless. In describing and analysing prose style it is also important to have a wide vocabulary at your disposal.

ACTIVITY 3:

Here is a short glossary of words critics have used to describe prose style, drawn from a useful book called *The College Handbook of Creative Writing* (DeMaria 1995). There are many, many more words one could use, of course. We have supplied the definition for the first few terms. Try to complete the list of definitions (using a dictionary where necessary), adding, where you can, examples of writers or types of writing which might exemplify such a style. Finally, find another five terms or more which might prove useful in describing prose style. You might want to use a thesaurus for this.

Descriptive term	Definition	Examples
abstract	theoretical, without reference to specifics	philosophical writing
analytical	inclined to examine things by studying their contents or parts	investigative writing, science writing, essays
anecdotal	incorporating anecdotes	some types of journalism
austere	stern, strict, frugal or unornamental	some modern poets such as T.S. Eliot or Ezra Pound
baroque	elaborate, grotesque and ornamental	Angela Carter
dispassionate	free from passion, uninfluenced by personal feelings	some forms of journalism, scientific reports
elegiac		
emphatic		
epigrammatical		
experimental		
flamboyant		
fluid		

Descriptive term	Definition	Examples
impressionistic		
journalistic		
lavish		
lyrical		
minimalist		
poetical		
sensuous		
staccato		
stilted		
stark		
verbose		
taut		
terse		

Here are two pieces of literary prose for you to consider. We have called the first piece conversational and the second impressionistic.

A conversational style

This is an extract from a comic novel written in the eighteenth century by Lawrence Sterne called *The Life and Opinions of Tristram Shandy* (1759–67). Tristram Shandy, the narrator who attempts to tell us his life story in the book, can never quite get to the point because he can always think of more stories to tell and other pieces of information he thinks we have to know before he moves forward in the plot. He also talks directly to the reader, even demanding sometimes that the reader go back and re-read a chapter when he thinks they have not been concentrating. In this passage he is trying to tell us about how his Uncle Toby was wounded in the groin in the siege of Namur:

> You will imagine, Madam, that my uncle Toby had contracted all this from this very source; – that he had spent a great part of his time in converse with your sex; and that, from a thorough knowledge of you, and the force of imitation which such fair examples render irresistible, he had acquired this amiable turn of mind.

I wish I could say so, – for unless it was with his sister-in-law, my father's wife and my mother, – my uncle Toby scarce exchanged three words with the sex in as many years; – no, he got it, Madam, by a blow. – A blow! – Yes, Madam, it was owing to a blow from a stone, broke off by a ball from the parapet of a horn-work at the siege of Namur, which struck full upon my uncle Toby's groin. – Which way could that affect it? The story of that, Madam, is long and interesting . . .

(Sterne 1972: 90–1)

ACTIVITY 4:

Why have we called this a 'conversational' style? What is conversational about it and why has Sterne used this way of writing? If you had to imitate it, how would you do it? How has Sterne used punctuation to enhance his style? What other kinds of writing might deploy a discursive style and why? Write up your responses to these questions as a short commentary and then try writing a few sentences of sports commentary in Sterne's version of a conversational style.

An impressionistic style

The early twentieth-century novelist Dorothy Richardson wrote a long novel in several volumes called *Pilgrimage*. This extract is from the volume called *Honeycomb*, which was published in 1917. Richardson was an experimental writer like many of her contemporaries, trying to find new ways of describing in particular the way in which the mind receives impressions from the outside world. She was influenced by the French writer Marcel Proust and to some extent by Impressionism in art. Visual impressionism, made popular by painters such as Renoir, Manet, Monet and Pissarro, was characterised by sketchiness and was radical and shocking in its time. The painters were trying to show that the way we see solid objects such as cathedrals or railway stations changes all the time as a result of the light and time of day. They too were concerned with the way in which the mind receives impressions. In the following passage Dorothy Richardson describes London as seen by her heroine as she moves through the streets:

The West End street . . . grey buildings rising on either side, angles sharp against the sky . . . softened angles of buildings against other buildings . . . high moulded angles soft as crumb, with deep undershadows . . . creepers fraying from balconies . . . strips of window blossoms across the buildings, scarlet, yellow, high up; a confusion of lavender and white pouching out along the dipping sill . . . a wash of green creeper up a white painted

house-front . . . patches of shadow and bright light . . . Sounds of visible
near things streaked and scored with broken light as they moved, led off
into untraced distant sounds . . . chiming together.

Wide golden streaming Regent Street was quite near. Some near narrow
street would lead into it.

Flags of pavement flowing – smooth clean grey squares and oblongs,
faintly polished, shaping and drawing away – sliding into each other . . .
I am part of the dense smooth clean paving stone . . . sunlit; gleaming under
dark winter rain; shining under warm sunlit rain, sending up a fresh stony
smell . . . always there . . . dark and light . . . dawn, stealing . . .

(Richardson 1979: 416)

ACTIVITY 5:

Why do you think this style is known as impressionistic? How has Richardson created it
(look at word choice and punctuation in particular)? What other kinds of writing might deploy
an impressionistic style? Where might it be inappropriate to use it? Write up your answers
in the form of a short report; then attempt an imitation of impressionist writing to describe
the street where you live.

Stylistic analysis

We have tried to demonstrate in this chapter the almost unlimited range of
prose styles used in writing. In considering style it is important to keep in
mind the use to which the writing will be put. Writers need to be flexible
and able to adapt what they write and the way they write to purpose and
context: spare, economical and stripped down for conventional essay and
formal letter writing, and more free-wheeling and impressionistic in diaries
and journals, for instance. In 1947 the French novelist, poet, mathemat-
ician and linguist Raymond Queneau published a strange and funny little
book called *Exercises de Style* (translated into English by Barbara Wright
in 1958 as *Exercises in Style* – Queneau 1998). In it Queneau retells a very
short and uneventful story about two men in Paris ninety-nine times, all
in different styles or genres. Titles include 'Spectral', 'Casual', 'Olfactory',
'Telegraphic', 'Awkward', 'Noble', 'Metaphorically'. Queneau claimed that
the book had been the result of his playful experiments with language over
a two-year period and that it should be seen as a 'linguistic rust-remover'.
Style, the book claims, is infinitely variable, and playing with it can be both
fascinating and funny.

There are times when simply choosing a word to describe a prose style is inadequate. In literary criticism sometimes a much more detailed and sustained analysis of prose style is needed which involves attending to the linguistic features of the chosen passage or passages much more closely. When talking about language like this it is important to be as specific as you can about sentence structure, choice of words, word combinations and patterns of sound and rhythm, and also remember that a piece of stylistic analysis should not just be a list of linguistic features but a consideration of why these linguistic features are used and what effects they create.

Here is a stylistic checklist based on one used in Rob Pope's *English Studies Handbook* (1998). In it Pope lists a series of questions which are useful in analysing the linguistic features of a particular piece of writing. They should not be used too slavishly or systematically, of course, but rather as a stimulus to thought and/or discussion. Not all the questions will be relevant to the particular piece of prose you are examining:

General
- What is the passage about and what is the writer trying to achieve?
- How would you describe the prose style in general terms?
- How does the prose style complement the supposed aims of the writer?

Word choice
- What sorts of vocabulary are being used?
- Is there a preference for certain words or word classes (adjectives, adverbs, etc.)?
- Is the register formal or colloquial and does it draw on particular specialist terms?
- What effects do these features create?
- Experiment by substituting, adding or deleting words.

Word combination
- Are there familiar collocations (recognisable word-clusters) or how much of it is strikingly new vocabulary?
- What kind of sentence structures does the writer use?
- Are there repetitions of individual words or of phrase or sentence structure?
- What tenses does the writer use and what frames of time, duration and frequency do they suggest?
- What kinds of verb does the writer use? Are they mostly active or passive verbs?
- What effects do these features create?
- Experiment with alternatives. What combinations have not been used but might have been?

Sound patterning and visual presentation
- What do you see, hear or infer with respect to:
  - stress, rhythm and intonation?
  - alliteration and assonance, rhyme or half-rhyme?
  - use of short or long vowel sounds?
  - distinctive features of punctuation?
- What effects do these features create?
- What alternatives might have been used? Experiment with other forms of sound patterning by rewriting certain sections.

(Based on Stylistic Checklist in Pope 1998: 259–61)

In order to give you an example of a more detailed piece of stylistic analysis, here are two extracts of non-fictional prose by two writers with very different prose styles, followed by an analysis of the first piece. The first passage is by the nineteenth-century artist, writer, critic and social commentator John Ruskin, who, in a section of his book *The Stones of Venice* (1851–53), takes us on an imaginary journey northwards from southern Europe to northern Europe to convince us that 'savageness' is an essential part of Gothic art. He describes Europe from the air in order to argue that northern art differs from southern art in part because of differences in the climate and landscape:

Let us, for a moment . . . imagine the Mediterranean lying beneath us like an irregular lake, and all its ancient promontories sleeping in the sun: here and there an angry spot of thunder, a grey stain of storm, moving upon the burning field; and here and there a fixed wreath of white volcano smoke, surrounded by its circle of ashes; but for the most part a great peacefulness of light, Syria and Greece, Italy and Spain, laid like pieces of a golden pavement into the sea-blue, chased as we stoop nearer to them, with bossy beaten work of mountain chains, and glowing softly with terraced gardens, and flowers heavy with frankincense, mixed among masses of laurel, and orange, and plumy palm, that abate with their grey-green shadows the burning of the marble rocks, and of the ledges of porphyry sloping under lucent sand. Then let us pass further towards the north, until we see the orient colours change gradually into a vast belt of rainy green, where the pastures of Switzerland, and poplar valleys of France, and dark forests of the Danube and Carpathian stretch from the mouths of the Loire to those of the Volga, seen through the clefts in grey swirls of rain cloud and flaky veils of the mist of the brooks, spreading low amongst the pasture lands: and then, further north still, to see the earth heave into mighty masses of leaden rock and heathy moor, bordering with a broad waste of gloomy purple that belt of field and wood, and splintering into irregular and grisly islands amidst the northern seas, beaten by storm, and chilled by ice drift, and tormented by furious pulses of contending tide, until the roots of the last forests fail from among the hill ravines, and the hunger of the north wind bites their peaks into barrenness; and, at last, the wall of ice, durable like iron, sets, deathlike, its white teeth against us out of the polar twilight.

(Ruskin 1995: 191)

Here is a stylistic analysis of the Ruskin piece. As you can see we have addressed many of the questions set out in Rob Pope's stylistic checklist and we have considered the linguistic features of the passage alongside questions about why such linguistic features have been chosen and what effect they create.

In this extract from Ruskin's Stones of Venice, Ruskin seeks to convince us that northern art differs from southern art because of essential differences in climate and landscape and their effect upon artistic sensibility. Ruskin's principal word here is 'savageness' and in this bird's-eye view of the landscape of Europe he demonstrates that northern Europe has a savageness of landscape which differs markedly from the soft shapes and colours of southern Europe. Ruskin's prose style is not just descriptive but highly poetic. As a painter as well as writer, Ruskin's description is not only detailed but also highly poetic as he creates something of a word painting to suggest to the reader the numerous similarities between European landscape and art.

Ruskin's description, as we would expect, is dominated by adjectives. The adjectives he uses to describe the south emphasise light, softness of colour and warmth, and the adjectives he uses to describe the north emphasise size ('mighty masses'), muted colours (grey and purple), rock ('splintering' and 'heaving') and dramatic emotions ('furious', 'tormented', 'beaten', 'chilled'). The words used to describe the south tend to use longer and softer vowel sounds whereas the words used to describe the north are more notable for their clipped and jagged consonantal sounds. The adjective–noun combinations are often highly unusual and poetic, as Ruskin uses alliteration and assonance to create evocative sounds and rhythms: 'lucent sand', 'grey swirls of rain cloud', 'grisly islands', and 'mighty masses', for instance. Ruskin also uses these adjective–noun combinations to create visual and painterly effects, particularly with colour and texture: 'flaky veils', 'grey stain of storm', 'gloomy purple', 'rainy green' and 'heathy moor'. In addition, Ruskin uses personification to describe the biting savagery of the arctic landscape: 'and the hunger of the north wind bites their peaks into barrenness; and, at last, the wall of ice, durable like iron, sets, deathlike, its white teeth against us out of the polar twilight'.

The extract is made up of two very long sentences (one describes the southern landscape and the other describes the northern landscape), punctuated by semi-colons and with clauses joined mostly through co-ordination. The lack of subordination in the sentences ensures that the sentences are easily comprehended. When read aloud, the long, co-ordinated sentences create a lyricism and fluency of sound which intensifies the poetic effects of the individual phrases and creates the illusion of swathes of colour and texture which are sweeping beneath us. The verbal structures are very simple in both sentences, allowing Ruskin to hang on the subject–verb structure ('Let us for a moment imagine...' and 'Let us pass further towards the north, until we see...') strings of phrases as he describes the various aspects of the climate and landscape. In addition, Ruskin adds a number of non-finite verb clauses to the main subject–verb structure to vary the descriptions of actions and states: 'tormented by', 'bordering with', 'chilled by', 'splintering into'. All the verbs are in the present tense to intensify the illusion that we are seeing all of these things here and now.

Ruskin's carefully crafted 'word painting' argues his case about the similarities between European art and landscape through both sight and sound. The long sentences and adjectival richness create an epic sweep wholly at one with the panoramic vision he offers us in the description. By using such a wide range of adjectives, Ruskin qualifies his description of northern art as 'savage' by showing that what he means by 'savage' is a series of related images, sounds and textures. Gothic art, for Ruskin, is 'heathy', jagged, splintered, irregular, leaden, grisly, mighty, and dominated by the drama of the northern climate.

ACTIVITY 6:

Write a short commentary on the analysis. Do you agree/disagree? Is there anything that you would want to change or add?

The second passage is by the twentieth-century journalist, writer and political commentator John Berger, who argues in this passage from his book *Ways of Seeing* (1972) that envy is an integral part of capitalism.

Glamour cannot exist without personal social envy being a common and widespread emotion. The industrial society which has moved towards democracy and then stopped half way is the ideal society for generating such an emotion. The pursuit of individual happiness has been acknowledged as a universal right. Yet the existing social conditions make the individual feel powerless. He lives in the contradiction between what he is and what he would like to be. Either he then becomes fully conscious of the contradiction and its causes, and so joins the political struggle for a full democracy which entails, amongst other things, the overthrow of capitalism; or else he lives, continually subject to an envy which, compounded with his sense of powerlessness, dissolves into recurrent day-dreams.

(Berger 1972: 148)

ACTIVITY 7:

Write an analysis of the extract from John Berger's *Ways of Seeing,* paying particular attention to the way in which linguistic features contribute to the effectiveness of the argument.

Personal styles and house styles

Whilst effective writing will usually carry something of the individuality of the writer, there are situations in which that personality needs to be more or less visible. For example, if you are writing a journal or a letter to an intimate friend, or an autobiographical account, or a thank-you speech, then your writing is likely to be effective by being fully personal and fully expressive of your thoughts and feelings.

There is, however, a wide range of more formal contexts in which a very personal style would not be appropriate. Journalists tend not to use 'I' in news reporting, for example, because their readers expect to read stories that are presented objectively. However, if the same journalist were asked to include witness testimony or to interview a number of ordinary people about their views on an election, those accounts would of course use 'I'. Similarly many businesses expect letters to clients to be formal and many even have a kind of format for such letters, a kind of 'house style', which can be very impersonal. Academic writing has a set of conventions which add up to something of a 'house style' – usually the style is formal, and sometimes, because it needs to persuade the reader of a particular viewpoint, the language will sound faintly legalistic, drawing on the language of proof and evidence. However, styles and house styles do change over time. Academic writing can be considerably enlivened by the use of 'I' where personal judgement and opinion are being expressed, and business letters are getting noticeably less formal and more 'we–you' in mode of address.

If you were employed as a writer of weather reports for a newspaper, you would first have to learn the 'house style' for weather reports. These tend to be similar in format the world over, although the following two reports taken from the internet, one from the UK and one from the United States, are rather different in the language they use. There are further differences of house style, of course, in spoken and written forms of language report.

General situation: A cold day in Scotland with showers, these falling as sleet and snow over the mountains, but the showers will become isolated during the afternoon. There will be a few scattered showers in Northern

Ireland, Wales and northern England but also some decent spells of sunshine. Elsewhere in England it will be a fresh day but it will be dry with plenty of sunshine in most parts.

(Daily Telegraph online, 15 October 1998)

October is usually one of the more pleasant months, from a weather standpoint, and Wednesday lived up to the billing. There were a few exceptions, however.

Rain moved into New England early on Wednesday. Although some pockets of heavy rain occurred, this event will be much less significant than the storm that deluged the region last weekend. While much of the area suffered through a damp Wednesday, Thursday's rain should focus in Northern New England. Southern New England can look forward to only a few showers. By Friday, the rain should be exiting the region, except for lingering showers over northern Maine.

Far to the west, a deepening trough of low pressure aloft will eventually spawn a vigorous storm on the Great Plains. The storm will begin to brew over Colorado, on Thursday, but probably won't reach maximum potency until Friday and Saturday. By then we expect wind, rain, thunder in the Plains and Upper Midwest. Thursday, the leading edge of this developing storm will spread showers and thunderstorms over parts of the Northern and Central Plains to the Upper Midwest. Showers and mountain snow will extend westward into sections of the northern Rockies.

The strengthening upper-level trough has prompted the National Weather Service to issue winter storm watches over parts of the West. Most of the heavy snow will fall late on Thursday into Friday, especially in Utah and Wyoming.

The combination of warm air aloft and an upper air disturbance brought some severe thunderstorms to parts of southern Minnesota and northern Iowa. A tornado was reported northeast of Des Moines, IA but there were no immediate reports of damage. These thunderstorms weakened rapidly as they moved eastward.

(The Weather Channel, Inc., 14 October 1998)

ACTIVITY 8:

Identify as many key phrases as you can which are typical of those used in the two weather reports and then analyse the differences between the British and American styles. Or imagine you are editor of one of the two organisations. You have a new member of staff who needs to learn the 'house style' of your weather reports so that s/he can write them. Write a short descriptive guide for either the British newspaper or the American Weather Channel.

ACTIVITY 9:

Listen to the morning news reports on either Radio 1 and Radio 4 or BBC1 and Channel Four's Big Breakfast. Record them if you can and play them back so that you can listen to them more carefully. Identify the house styles of the two different news rooms. What language do they use and why? Choose one of the two house styles and write a fictional news item in that particular style. Add a commentary explaining what you were trying to do.

House styles used in business are often very impersonal. Impersonality has its place when the writing needs to appear objective and professional, but when impersonality is taken too far it can lead to dehumanised writing. Many of the brochures and reports we read in the world of business are full of passive sentences working hard to erase any personalities behind the scenes. The 'house style' or the rule book is often very impersonal. Look at the following example from a university *Rules and Regulations* manual for students:

> Where a sponsor is a government agency, credit facilities will be given where confirmation or a fee payment liability has been received by completion of Form F984 or a letter from the organisation concerned. Such documentation must be presented at Registration.

> (Anglia Polytechnic University 1998: 47)

The passage can be translated into a less formal style in the following way:

> If your grant hasn't arrived, but you've got a form from your local authority saying that they *are* going to pay it, then we'll still let you register, if you show us the form as proof.

Passive verb constructions are used throughout this passage: 'credit facilities will be given' and 'confirmation has been received' (the active construction would be 'we will give you credit facilities' and 'when your funding authority gives us confirmation'). Because the writer has used passive sentences, it is impossible to tell who will be giving the credit facilities because the passage says only 'credit facilities will be given' – it doesn't say who by. And who should the student show the letter (the confirmation of fee payment liability) to? The passage is deliberately impersonal because the university concerned cannot say that the student should show their letter of confirmation to Mr Smith or that they should apply to Ms Jones for credit because the person responsible for gathering such letters or giving credit will be different in each department and will change regularly as staff leave and are replaced. Passives obfuscate but are sometimes necessary and unavoidable. They do, however, become a problem if they are used excessively in any piece of writing.

ACTIVITY 10:

The following is an extract from the Fifth Amendment of the US constitution. Rewrite the extract using a 'we–you' mode of informal address. How does your new version compare with the original? What has been lost and/or gained in the rewriting?

> No person shall be held to answer for a capital, or other infamous crime, unless on a presentment or indictment of a Grand Jury, except in cases arising in the land or naval forces, or in the militia, when in actual service, in time of war or public danger; nor shall any person be subject for the same offence to be twice put in jeopardy of life or limb; nor shall be compelled in any criminal case to be a witness against himself; nor be deprived of his life, liberty, or property, without due process of law; nor shall private property be taken for public use without just compensation.

There is another kind of impersonality of style which can sometimes appear in formal or business writing. In such writing, writers, often in positions of authority, avoid saying things directly because to say them directly would be uncomfortable. Here, for instance, is a fictional memo sent from a board of directors to all employees:

> In accordance with the company's financial strategies for 1997, financial priorities have been identified and measures have been taken to ensure that the company meets its commitments to 1 per cent growth over the next financial year. These measures include a strategic commitment to selective contraction of labour costs.

Essentially the memo announces that there will be jobs lost through the company's commitment to increased profit. The passive sentences work to hide the person responsible for making the decision. Who has taken the measures? Who has identified the priorities? Why did they think that increasing the profit margin by a further 1 per cent was more important than the effect of redundancy on a number of employees? All humanity has been lost in this passage – all the managers behind the decision and all the workers who will suffer redundancy have been erased. The writer is hiding behind passive sentences and other kinds of impersonal constructions (such as 'there are reasons to believe', 'it is clear that', 'the fact of the matter is'). Listen to politicians being interviewed on the radio or television and you will be able to collect a number of these impersonal constructions.

ACTIVITY 11:

You are the head teacher of a large primary school and you have just received details from the local education authority about the new literacy hour which the government requires you to institute in all your classes. This will require that all teachers restructure their classroom timetables in order to make time for the literacy hour (all children must have structured reading instruction and practice for one hour every day). You know that your staff are under a great deal of pressure with administration commitments and large class sizes. You know they are likely to find that the literacy hour will increase their workloads even further, requiring them to abandon or reschedule other class activities. However, you do think the government initiative is a good one and would like your teachers to respond well to the idea from the start.

You have decided to circulate a letter to the teachers in the school designed to introduce them to the idea. Write one version of the memo in a heavily impersonal style (using passive constructions). Write a second version in a style which is more personal and direct and which reveals more of you and your views, but still retains some of the formality required by your position as head teacher.

ACTIVITY 12:

Find a piece of writing which has a distinctive 'house style' (for example, a guide book, a tourist brochure, an estate agent's description of a house, descriptions of programmes in the *Radio Times*, a recipe in a particular cookery book) and make up your own version following the house style closely. Write at least two drafts and attach a short commentary to each saying what you were trying to do with your version in relation to the house style of the original and how you think you have made improvements from one draft to another

ACTIVITY 13:

Write a journal entry every day for a week, describing the events of each day. Try to write each one in a different style: for example, ornate, discursive, plain, impersonal, colloquial, rhythmic, poetic, impressionistic. Attach a short paragraph to each saying what you were trying to do and what the style achieves in terms of effect.

Summary

In this chapter we have looked at:

- definitions of style
- terminology for describing style
- stylistic analysis
- imitating and rewriting prose styles
- personal and impersonal styles of address
- house styles.

References

Allot, M. (1973) *Novelists on the Novel*. London: Routledge.

Anglia Polytechnic University Higher Education Corporation (1998) *Rules, Regulations and Procedures for Students*, 5th edn. Chelmsford and Cambridge: Anglia Polytechic University.

Berger, John (1972) *Ways of Seeing*. Harmondsworth: Penguin.

DeMaria, R. (1995) *The College Handbook of Creative Writing*. New York: Harcourt Brace.

Heaney, Seamus (1980) 'Feeling into Words' in *Preoccupations: Selected Prose 1968–1978*. London: Faber and Faber.

Milic, Louis (1970) 'Connectives in Swift's Prose Style' in D. Freeman (ed.), *Linguistics and Literary Style*. New York: Holt, Rinehart and Winston.

Pope, Rob (1998) *The English Studies Handbook*. London: Routledge.

Queneau, R. (1998) *Exercises in Style* [1947], trans. Barbara Wright. London: John Calder.

Richardson, Dorothy (1979) *Honeycomb* from *Pilgrimage*, Vol. 1 [1917]. London: Virago.

Ruskin, John (1995), 'The Savageness of Gothic Architecture' in *The Stones of Venice* [1851–53]. London: J.M. Dent.

Sterne, Lawrence (1972) *Tristram Shandy* [1759–67]. Harmondsworth: Penguin.

Woolf, Virginia (1929) *A Room of One's Own*. London: Hogarth Press.

Woolf, Virginia (1963) *Orlando* [1928]. Harmondsworth: Penguin.

Styles in context

Anna Snaith

I n the last chapter we looked at a variety of prose styles in order to demonstrate how styles change according to usage – with place, setting, time and the audience being addressed. This chapter will explore in more detail the ways in which such contexts determine the kind of prose styles we use for different kinds of writing. In particular it will consider the importance of an awareness of register and discourse worlds, and examine the idea of appropriate word choice. It will also provide you with a range of different linguistic terms to use when analysing the styles of the many varieties of writing around you.

We do not read or write texts in a vacuum; rather, they are both created and received in specific social contexts which help to determine their meaning. Our understanding of any kind of written text relies upon its context: who it is written by, who it is addressed to or written for, where we read it, and how it is represented visually. When we read a text we take all these factors into account, even if only subconsciously. We often become so used to the contexts of certain kinds of written texts – for example, a newspaper, graffiti, a menu, a road sign, a novel or a letter – that we can predict many of the words to be found in them. This means that when we come to read that particular text, we arrive with expectations and have already made assumptions about what we are about to read. For example, look at the following four phrases and try to determine what kind of context (written or spoken) they might have been used in or what kind of text they might have been taken from:

Clinton allies urge him to testify
Are you ready to order?
Hands up anyone who knows the answer
A low pressure front will bring rain

The first phrase is a newspaper headline. We can guess that it comes from a broadsheet rather than a tabloid newspaper as its treatment of the Bill Clinton/Monica Lewinsky affair is more objective than it is sensational. (The headline actually appeared in *The Times* on 28 July 1998.) The second phrase could be heard in a restaurant, while the context of the third is likely to be a primary school classroom. The final example is a weather forecast and probably a spoken, television forecast rather than a written one because of the use of both a full grammatical sentence and a full explanation for the rain. A written forecast often tends to be expressed in short phrases such as 'dull and drizzly' or 'light, variable winds' rather than full sentences.

In many cases context is essential for determining the meaning of a written or spoken text, since words can have different meanings depending on where they are found. A sign saying 'Delivery Room' in a maternity ward, for example, would have a very different meaning from a similar sign in a postal sorting office! And the word 'Exit' has the same meaning, but indicates very different actions, when read as a sign above a door or on a computer. Part of creating meaning from language, then, depends not just on understanding the words themselves – the lexis or diction of a text – but also on understanding shared social contexts. Such contexts can be complicated by the fact that they vary according to regional, cultural and racial differences. The phrase 'way out', for example, has one primary meaning in Britain (exit) and rather a different one in North America (eccentric, offbeat). An American in Britain, however, would have no trouble realising that the sign meant 'exit' because of the context: the fact that it was a sign and that it was over a door.

Given all of this, then, you need to think carefully about the idea of context when you write as well as when you read. Who is the audience you are addressing your written text to, and what is your relationship to that audience? Should the text be formal or informal? Is it a business letter, a love letter, an essay, a memo or a report? In order to ensure effective communication, these questions need to be carefully considered as the answers will help determine your word choice and subsequently the style and tone of the piece.

Register

Register is the term used for the range of styles of written or spoken language which are used in particular contexts and circumstances. It is a key term in language study. In our social lives register is ever-present in that we adjust the way we speak or write according to the need for formal or informal expression. This, of course, depends upon context and audience. Think, for example, of the number of times in one day that you alter the register of your speech depending on who you are talking to: your bank manager, your mother, your friends. Registers are not merely formal or informal, but include many subtle gradations in between these, and it is a mark of a person's competence in communication skills if they are able to switch between registers appropriately and effectively. It is helpful to think of register in terms of a spectrum of formal and informal language not just an either/or. For example the spectrum of words:

inebriated   drunk   tipsy   pissed

all mean approximately the same thing, but the one you might choose to use would be selected for its appropriateness to the context in which you were writing or speaking. You are more likely to hear the word 'inebriated' in court and the word 'pissed' in a pub. Register does not just refer to word choice either, as other language choices contribute to the final effect of that spectrum from formal to informal, such as grammatical structures, length of sentences and so on. Register is therefore another term which is used to indicate variety of language and is a way of describing the vast differences in the styles of the numerous texts that we read or the speech acts that we speak/hear. Tone, style and word choice can be altered to suit a particular situation through radical adjustment or fine-tuning, and often this is related to degrees of formality. In any given situation, however, we tend to be consistent in our use of a particular register and not to shift register suddenly, although this can be used for comic or shocking effect (see the section on humour below).

Register is determined by lexical (word choice) and grammatical elements, as well as by the following contextual factors:

- the purpose of the text we are writing (the field)
- our relationship with the addressee/s (the tenor)
- the medium of communication (the mode).

In discussing register, therefore, we need to look at meaning, style and context together. In other words, we need to analyse what the text says, how it says it, and where and when it says it. Register is created by the relationship between these elements of a text.

There are two other terms which we can use to help describe a particular register – closed and open registers. Documents such as gas bills or bus timetables usually have closed registers because they are tightly structured and leave little room for ambiguity of meaning. They give the information required clearly and directly. The language of air traffic control is often cited as another example of a closed register because the language used is restricted and fixed, and the safety of aircraft relies on this fixity – the controllers should not start discussing their upcoming holidays or last night's football match if the plane is to land safely! Open registers, on the other hand, are much less fixed and are more open to interpretation. Examples of written texts which often use open registers are newspapers, fiction and poetry, which have a more variable range of language. There is, of course, a sliding scale concerning how open a particular register can be: the conversation between a dentist and his/her patient, for example, is likely to be more predictable than a chat between friends, but less predictable than that between a bus conductor and a passenger. Texts or speech acts – a personal letter or a conversation, for example – can take any number of forms and use a wide variety of styles from the very formal to the very informal.

We also need to consider the political dimension of register, since a particular register can be used to exercise power and/or authority over others. For example, a formal register can sometimes be used to intimidate in an oral or written context – at a job interview, perhaps, or in a threatening letter. Any distinctive register can also be used to alienate or exclude the reader/listener or to create a sense of exclusivity within a particular group. The choice of a particular register can therefore be a highly political act as the use of formal or informal registers can be fundamental in the part language plays in maintaining and perpetuating the distinctness of certain systems, groups and social classes. We will discuss this issue further in the following chapter on writing in a clear English style, but for now, can you think of any examples of this exclusivity or alienation linked to register from your own experience?

When using the term 'register', it is important to keep in mind the huge range of styles and contexts to which it refers, and that it is a term which needs to be used loosely rather than prescriptively. For example, to talk about the register of reports could imply that there is one fixed formula for all reports. However, of course, there are several possible types of report which might include:

- a government policy document
- a clothes buyer's report to his/her boss on the coming season
- a report to university staff on the introduction of a new course
- a book report by a GCSE English student
- a report on a patient by a psychiatrist.

These different reports would almost certainly have different registers. Which do you think would be the most formal and which the most informal? Why? What factors do you need to take into account when making your decision?

The same point about the variety of registers in reports is true for other types of writing, such as business letters, memos, etc. The difference in register will depend specifically upon the purpose of the document. Again, therefore, we need to return to the idea of context and consider, for example, the type of company, area of work or experience for which the letter or memo is being written. Even the register of a weather forecast, which we looked at in Chapter 1, varies according to whether it is heard on television or radio or printed in a newspaper, on which channel or station it is broadcast or in which newspaper it is printed, and whether it is a specialist forecast such as the shipping forecast. Go back to this exercise in Chapter 1 and reconsider the forecasts printed there – how would you describe the registers which are being used? Are they open or closed? How formal or informal are they?

Another point to consider when using the term register is the similarity between register and other terms such as genre (text type). One might ask what the difference is between the genre and the register of a letter. There is certainly an overlap between the two, but whereas genre simply differentiates between various kinds of texts (novel, letter, play, poem), register also takes into account the style, tone and diction of the particular text. In the single genre of the short story, for example, writers are able to employ a wide variety of registers. Below are three examples of different texts. Example 1 is an extract from a book contract, Example 2 is from a tourism brochure for short breaks in Lewes, Sussex, and Example 3 is a personal thank-you note. Read the three pieces through and think about how you would describe the registers being used. What are the differences?

Example 1

Where the Author dies or becomes completely incapacitated or incapable of performing under the terms of this Agreement during the course of this Agreement the Publisher shall be entitled to be given copies of all notes, manuscripts or other materials relating to the Work and to continue to publish the Work. If insufficient material exists for the publication on the Author's death the Publisher may select a third party to complete the Work the cost of such commissioning being deductible from payments due to the Author's estate.

Example 2

At the heart of the South Downs, Lewes District's inordinately beautiful landscape provides some of England's most appealing and unspoilt Chalkland scenery. A colourful County town and two thousand years of rich history combine with dramatic coastline, undulating hills, and swathes of verdant farmland peppered with picturesque villages, to ensure that the Lewes area is a perfect base for today's discerning visitors.

Example 3

Dear Laura,
Thanks loads for dinner last night. Great to see you and catch up. Glad things are working out with your new job. Have a brill holiday – don't get too burnt! – and see ya when you get back. Lots of love, Nicole.

When we read these three extracts our sense of their meaning is created by envisioning their context: a legal document, a glossy brochure and a hastily written note. We are already making expectations about the types of language and degrees of formality we will find. Let's consider the register of each in more detail.

Even though the subject of Example 1 is the author's death, we expect dry, formal legal language as this is part of a legal contract. The register is created through formal diction (e.g. 'incapacitated') and convoluted or archaic sounding syntax (e.g. 'the cost of such commissioning being deductible'). Legal documents must leave no room for misunderstanding so everything is spelt out in full, hence the repetition of key terms (e.g. 'Author', 'Work') to avoid any ambiguity. Writing dealing with death is often emotional – think of the ways in which obituaries are written, for example, or accounts of death scenes in fiction – but here the purpose of the writing is to set out rules so the treatment is objective.

Knowing that the context of Example 2 is a glossary tourism brochure, we would expect heightened, energetic descriptions which attempt to sell the area to the reader by emphasising its attractiveness and uniqueness. Indeed, the register here is typical of advertising. The use of superlatives such as 'most appealing and unspoilt', and intensified adjectives such as 'inordinately beautiful' rather than just 'beautiful', is intended to persuade the reader of the worth of the product (the area). In many ways the area is being presented as ideal or 'perfect'. Alliteration (the repetition of the initial consonant in two or more words as in 'peppered with picturesque') is also used, as in many written adverts, to heighten the attractiveness of the sound of the language and hence the object being described, while flattery is used to manipulate the reader: a tourist who picks Lewes for a holiday destination is 'discerning'.

Example 3 shows an informal register, where attention to grammar and sophisticated vocabulary is not a priority. The tone is chatty and closer to spoken language than the preceding examples. The use of ellipsis (e.g. 'Great to see you' instead of 'It was great to see you') creates this effect, as does the use of contractions (e.g. 'don't'), the dashes and exclamation mark, and the slang form of you ('ya').

As we have been suggesting, register is intricately related to the particular situation in which a text is written and read. A writer should think very carefully about the audience for which s/he is writing and make certain that the register is appropriate. Below are two letters, each of them containing the same information but having very different registers. Read them through and think carefully about the question of appropriateness. Is the register of one letter more appropriate than the other? Why?

Letter 1

Cooper and Smyth, Ltd
125 Aldgate Road
London N4 1PT
020-8372-6594

Ms P. Linklater
52 Oldbury Road
London, N4 5SF

2 August 2000

Dear Ms Linklater,
I am writing to inform you of the success of your application for the position of Office Administrator for the company Cooper and Smyth, Inc. Your contract will be for two years in the first instance, with a six month probation period. Please telephone our office and we can arrange a meeting to discuss further particulars with you. We look forward to hearing from you.

Yours sincerely,
Margaret Cooper

Letter 2

Cooper and Smyth, Ltd
125 Aldgate Road
London, N4 1PT
020-8372-6594

Ms Linklater
52 Oldbury Road
London, N4 5SF

August 2, 2000

Yo Trish,
Congrats! Great work! You were numero uno candidate for the job of office runaround. It's for 2 years, with a 6 month testing period. Hope you can hack it! Give us a bell and we'll fix up to have a chinwag and go and sink a few pints.

Bye for now,
Maggie

Although this is an extreme example, it demonstrates that you, as writers, need to think about the register which will suit your audience. Letter 2 contains the same information as Letter 1, but the register is obviously far too informal for a professional business letter. The language used – mostly a mixture of colloquialisms and slang – and the informal grammatical structures and contractions are completely inappropriate for an employer writing to a prospective employee, implying a familiarity which does not exist. Letter 1, on the other hand, maintains a register throughout which is formal yet polite and friendly. Go back through this first letter and identify any specific language or grammatical elements which you think help to achieve this effect.

ACTIVITY 1:

As organiser of your university's Literary Society, you are in charge of arranging a theatre trip for fifty undergraduates to see a play in London and you have to write a letter to the head of the English department to tell him/her of the details. You have decided to go to see a production of *Twelfth Night*, for which the tickets cost £13 each. The coach hire will be another £75 and you want to arrange for everyone to eat out afterwards. You therefore need to ask for financial support in the form of subsidy from the department. Write the letter to your head of department (a) in a formal register and (b) in an informal register, making sure that you include all the information in both letters. Then write a short paragraph describing what language choices you made in order to create the register.

ACTIVITY 2:

Analyse the register of the following synopsis of the movie *Grease*, written for its re-release. Look at diction, tone and syntax, as well as considering the purpose of the text and its context in a fashion magazine. Make detailed notes. If you are working in groups, compare your notes and ideas with those of the other students in your group. Choose the best points and write them up in the form of a short report.

Hot from the success of *Saturday Night Fever*, the svelte, bequiffed and beguiling John Travolta had a second huge hit with this cheesy but likeable musical, which is being re-released to mark its twentieth anniversary. John Travolta and Olivia Newton-John star as the 1950s high-school lovers Danny and Sandy – he is besotted, trying desperately to maintain his 'cool' image, she, a wet newcomer, is pushed and prodded by the jealous Rizzo (Stockard Channing). The jokes are excruciating, the songs absurd and the dance numbers mostly shambolic, but the film survives through sheer energy, the undeniable class of Travolta and huge amounts of tongue in cheek. 'Stranded at the drive-in, branded a fool, what will they say, Monday at school?' Say no more.

(*Marie-Claire*, July 1998)

Word choice

In this section we are going to look at the effects of word choice and the relationship between word choice and register. We can start by thinking about how we choose between words which appear to refer to the same thing. For example, if we look in a thesaurus under the word 'fashion' we get the following list of words:

fashion, style, mode, vogue, fad, rage, craze, dernier cri, cry

These words are classed as synonyms, which means that they are words which have the same meaning. We might want to pause here, however, and ask ourselves whether two words ever have exactly the same meaning. Surely the answer is no, because synonymous words often have slightly different connotations. Connotations are the associated meanings which are aroused by or suggested by our reading or hearing specific words. For example, consider the word 'cat'. The core, referential meaning of this word (called the denotation) is 'a feline quadruped'. The associative connotations of the word, however, depending on how you think of cats, might include 'friend', 'comfort', 'independence', 'hunter', etc. If we then return to the list of words for 'fashion', we can see one way in which different registers are created, since although these words are supposedly synonymous, there are shades of difference in their meanings. It is true that all of these words denote a way of dressing, acting, decorating one's home, etc. which is considered up-to-date. Yet 'style' could suggest a distinctive way of dressing, which is not necessarily in fashion. 'Mode' suggests a more sophisticated height of fashion than 'fad' or 'craze', which have a more populist connotation and indicate a short-lived trend. 'Dernier cri' and 'cry' (as in 'all the cry') indicate the latest item in fashion. 'Fad', 'rage' and 'craze' sound more colloquial, suggesting a younger market, whereas 'mode' and 'vogue' are more formal in register. 'Dernier cri' and 'cry' sound distinctly out of date to a modern reader. This list clearly shows how a group of similar words can have slightly different meanings and how words can also go in and out of fashion! Often when a word is 'reclaimed' by a different group at a different time, its meaning is also changed. Consider, for example, 'wicked' as used by certain groups of young people in the early 1990s as opposed to its more conventional use, or the way in which the word 'gay' has altered its meaning in the late twentieth century.

When you are writing, therefore, you are constantly choosing from lists of similar words. The more conscious you are about this process and the longer the lists are from which you choose, the more interesting, effective and varied your writing style can become. Make sure you have a dictionary and a thesaurus to hand when writing and think carefully about the words you draw upon, always considering if there are more appropriate or interesting ones you could use. The English language is extremely rich and varied – try to use it to its full potential.

ACTIVITY 3:

Below are three lists of synonyms. Think about them carefully and consider the variations in meaning. Are some words more current or archaic (antiquated, no longer in ordinary use) than others? Are there some which you have trouble defining? Try to arrange the words on a scale from the very formal to the very informal. (Use a dictionary or thesaurus if you're stuck!) Then produce your own set of synonymous words and write a short paragraph describing the differences in meaning as we did for the list of fashion words above.

gift, present, favour, boon, largesse, gratuity
food, victuals, viands, provisions, comestibles, nourishment, sustenance, nutriment, fodder, forage
error, slip, blunder, mistake, faux pas, bull, howler, cock-up

ACTIVITY 4:

This activity will help you consider the idea of word choice further. The table below categorises words according to degrees of formality – formal, informal, colloquial, slang. 'Intoxicated', for example, has a more formal register and can be found in police or medical reports. As we said earlier, 'pissed' is much more the kind of word you might hear (or use) in a very informal situation! Fill in the gaps and then add a row of words of your own at the bottom.

Formal	Semi-formal	Colloquial	Slang
intoxicated	drunk	tipsy	pissed
gentleman	man	bloke	
police constable			
			snuffed it
		cash	
	insane		
incarcerated			
lady			

Another important factor to note about register is that it depends upon making word choices about open class words rather than closed class words. Closed class words – articles, prepositions, conjunctions, pronouns – are the main function words which remain the same in any given situation or text. They are used to form the basic syntactic structures of sentences and do not change according to formality or content. Open class words, on the other hand, are those words – verbs, nouns, adjectives, adverbs – which have a referential function, referring to objects and experiences. These are the word classes which can be added to and changed as language alters over time, through the process of neologism (the invention of new words). They are therefore the groups of words where a writer or speaker has a range from which to choose – whether to say 'flat', ' apartment' or 'domicile', for example, or whether to say 'water closet', 'toilet' or 'loo'. Open class words comprise the bulk of the lexicon of the language.

ACTIVITY 5:

Below is an extract from a short story published around the same time as *A Portrait of the Artist*, Franz Kafka's *Metamorphosis* (*Die Verwandlung*, 1916). It is a terrifying and disturbing story as the protagonist, Gregor Samsa, wakes up one morning and has to deal with the metamorphosis that has occurred to him during the night. Below are the opening paragraphs. Part of the horror of this scene comes from the way in which the effects of the transformation are described in such a deadpan manner. There are several registers at work here which are constantly colliding against one another (horror, domestic, business, etc). Work through the passage identifying how these registers work and examine the effects of word choice and sentence structure. If you are working in groups, discuss your ideas together. Make a list of your ten most interesting ideas and observations and write these up as a short report.

As Gregor Samsa awoke one morning from uneasy dreams he found himself trans-formed in his bed into a gigantic insect. He was lying on his hard, as it were armour-plated, back and when he lifted his head a little he could see his dome-like brown belly divided into stiff arched segments on top of which the bed-quilt could hardly keep in position and was about to slide off completely. His numerous legs, which were pitifully thin compared to the rest of his bulk, waved helplessly before his eyes.

What has happened to me? he thought. It was no dream. His room, a regular human bedroom, only rather too small, lay quiet between the four familiar walls. Above the table on which a collection of cloth samples was unpacked and spread out – Samsa was a commercial traveller – hung the picture which he had recently cut out of an illustrated magazine and put into a pretty gilt frame. It showed a lady, with a fur cap on and a fur stole, sitting upright and holding out to the spectator a huge fur muff into which the whole of her forearm had vanished.

Gregor's eyes turned next to the window, and the overcast sky – one could hear raindrops beating on the window gutter – made him quite melancholy. What about sleeping a little longer and forgetting all this nonsense, he thought, but it could not be done, for he was accustomed to sleep on his right side and in his present condition he could not turn himself over. However violently he forced himself towards his right side he always rolled on to his back again. He tried it at least a hundred times, shutting his eyes to keep from seeing his struggling legs, and only desisted when he began to feel in his side a faint dull ache he had never experienced before.

O God, he thought, what an exhausting job I've picked on! Travelling about day in, day out. It's much more irritating work than doing the actual business in the warehouse, and on top of that there's the trouble of constant travelling, or worrying about train connections, the bed and irregular meals, casual acquaintances that are always new and never become intimate friends. The devil take it all! He felt a slight itching up on his belly; slowly pushed himself on his back nearer to the top of the bed so that he could lift his head more easily; identified the itching place which was surrounded by many small white spots the nature of which he could not understand, and made to touch it with a leg, but drew the leg back immediately, for the contact made a cold shiver run through him.

(Kafka 1978: 9–10)'

Another useful term when talking about word choice is collocation. Words collocate when they commonly appear next to or near one another in texts. They can be two words which are commonly and predictably found together, such as 'meteoric rise' or 'golden handshake', or a phrase such as 'kick the bucket', 'bury the hatchet' or 'pull one's leg'. (Such phrases are also called idioms – that is, their meaning is not easily determined from the meanings of the constituent parts. To 'kick the bucket', for example, means more than just hitting it with your foot!) Collocation means that some words will sound right together while others will sound unfamiliar. This unfamiliarity can be used to effect, however, to make one's writing sound fresh or unusual.

ACTIVITY 6:

This exercise demonstrates the predictability of word pairs and groups. Match the word on the left to the corresponding word on the right. Some will be more obvious than others. Are there any which you are unable to match straight away? Are there any which collocate with more than one other? What does this tell you about language and collocation?

impeccably	prices
pious	fatale
spill	butter
unforeseen	amok
femme	hope
running	circumstance
soaring	dressed
rancid	value

auspicious	your socks up
intrinsic	the beans
pull	event

At this stage you should make sure that you understand all the terms we have introduced in this chapter. If there are any in the list below that you are unclear about, check them in the text above, or the glossary at the back of this book.

- register
- field
- tenor
- mode
- genre
- open register
- closed register
- synonym
- connotation
- open class words
- closed class words
- collocation.

Discourse worlds

The term discourse world (also called discourse community) refers to a type of language (written or spoken) used by a particular group of people in a particular context. Often this specialist language represents a specific area of knowledge or experience, and therefore the words are usually technical terms or phrases related to the occupation or interest group. Examples of discourse worlds would be the language of computer experts, the legal profession, motorbike enthusiasts, bird watchers, estate agents or literary critics. Discourse worlds are related to register since the use of consistently technical or specialised language in, for example, an advertisement, report or business letter might be said to contribute to the register of that particular text.

We need to think about the political implications of discourse worlds, as we did with register. Discourse worlds, even more than register, can be exclusive and can alienate readers or listeners who are not familiar with the terms used. However, specialised language can also ensure efficient and effective intercommunication between members of the discourse community. They share specialised knowledge, therefore there is no need to explain the terms used. Indeed, the use of technical terms can often work as a kind of shorthand between those who understand them. Very often members of a discourse community share common goals or values within a particular area.

However, this use of language can seem impenetrable to those not 'in the know'. Awareness of audience is crucial here then. As writers, you need to gauge how familiar your readers will be with the terms you use. Are you writing an academic essay and therefore there is no need to explain certain literary or scientific terms, or are you writing for a more general audience who would be put off by such terms?

Alternatively, the specialised language of discourse worlds may sometimes be called jargon (this is usually used to mean the excessive use of over-specialised words). There is clearly a relative judgement here: whether a television manual is too jargon-filled to be useful, for example, or whether academic language has replaced clarity with jargon are questions which are often up for debate. Again, we will return to these issues in the next chapter on writing in a clear English style.

As with the term 'register', it is important that the term 'discourse world' is used loosely if we are not to overgeneralise. A discourse world could be that of an English department, a marketing company, or a dance class. To some extent, all English departments, all marketing companies and all dance classes will work within the same discourse world, but then again each individual group will have its own favoured terms and phrases.

The use of discourse worlds is particularly important in advertising. In computer and car adverts particularly, specialised and technical language is often used to give the impression of expertise and authority. Advertisers reason that such use of language makes you trust the company and the product – that is, that they must know what they're talking about!

ACTIVITY 7:

Here are three examples of discourse worlds in use. Example 1 is from a book on gardening, Example 2 is from an iMac computer advertisement, and Example 3 is from an advertisement for a house in an estate agent's brochure. Analyse the discourse worlds at work, paying particular attention to word choice, phrasing and tone. Write up your points in a short report which compares the three pieces. Then find another short piece of advertising and imitate the language that is peculiar to that particular discourse world (you might want to look at car adverts, for instance). Add a short commentary describing how you went about the task and what elements you were drawing upon in your own piece.

Example 1

Propagation: By division or offsets in spring or early summer, or by seed. Sow ripe seed in slightly humus-rich, soil-based compost in autumn in a cold frame, and germination will usually take place in spring.

(Buczacki 1994: 34)

Example 2

Our new iMac DV models include Apple's breakthrough digital video technology, so you can play DVD films or connect your digital camcorder to create your own pro-quality home movies complete with special effects.

...Blazing peripherals. The iMac DV model has superfast FireWire built in, so you can directly connect to high-speed devices like digital camcorders and external disk drives.

...Point and plug. A new doorless side panel gives you easy access to the built-in 56K modem, Ethernet, USB and high-speed FireWire ports.

...Now hear this. iMac is the first computer to integrate Harman Kardon's new micro-speakers, which deliver ultra-clean sound across a wide dynamic range.

(iMac advertisement, November 1999)

Example 3

Dble room to let in beautiful shared det. house. F/furnished. All mod cons. Good order. Private access. wc/shower. cooking fac. d/glazing. gas ch. Quiet location. Riverside views. 10 mins station and c/c. Convenient M1/M25. Suit n/s couple. Min 6 mths. Refs/Deps req. £400pcm + elec.

Humour

Much humour revolves around the use (and misuse) of register. This misalignment of content and situation (i.e. an overly formal register for an informal situation or vice versa) draws on the incongruity of the situation. We laugh because the words (spoken or written) are unexpected.

Copying the register of a particular text or a certain writer is called pastiche. You could write a passage in the style of Charles Dickens or a Mills and Boon novel, for instance, drawing upon typical vocabulary, grammatical structures and sound effects, as well as typical subject matters and situations. Pastiche can also be produced on a larger scale, such as John Fowles's *The French Lieutenant's Woman* (1969) and A.S. Byatt's *Possession* (1990), which are both pastiches of the Victorian novel. In general, pastiche does not necessarily set out to deride the text that is being drawn upon; rather, producing a pastiche of somebody's work can be seen as a way of praising it.

On the other hand, copying the register of a text for the purpose of satirising or critiquing it is called parody and is often done for humorous effects. Some parodies mimic only the form and content of the original text, while others copy the writer's style as well in what can be described as a form of literary caricature.

Another form of humour related to register is malapropism. This is the substitution of a word in a sentence or familiar phrase with one which sounds similar but which has an inappropriate meaning. Use of malapropisms can suggest that the speaker or writer is trying to use a more formal register than he or she is comfortable with. The character Mrs Malaprop in Sheridan's play *The Rivals* (1775) makes extensive use of this trope, as her name would suggest. Sheridan would have taken his character's name from the French phrase 'mal à propos' (meaning 'inappropriate') and from Sheridan's usage we have derived the term malapropism. A more contemporary example of a Mrs Malaprop is Julia Brogan on the TV soap opera *Brookside*. The following sentences illustrate malapropisms.

> The woman fell down the stairs and lay prostitute at the bottom.
> My neighbour has a lovely muriel on her bathroom wall.

ACTIVITY 8:

Below is a parody of Shakespeare's sonnet XVIII, 'Shall I compare thee to a summer's day?' First read the original through carefully, making notes in your study groups on subject, form, diction, imagery, etc. Then analyse the parody by Peter Titheradge on your own, before discussing your analyses in groups. How has the writer parodied the content and style of Shakespeare's sonnet? How does he create a blend of discourse worlds in his parody? Are there any serious points Titheradge is trying to make? Write a short commentary summarising your responses to these questions.

Shakespeare's Sonnet XVIII

Shall I compare thee to a summer's day?
Thou art more lovely and more temperate.
Rough winds do shake the darling buds of May,
And summer's lease hath all too short a date.
Sometime too hot the eye of heaven shines,
And often is his gold complexion dimmed;
And every fair from fair sometime declines,
By chance or nature's changing course untrimmed.
But thy eternal summer shall not fade,
Nor lose possession of that fair thou ow'st,
Nor shall Death brag thou wand'rest in his shade,
When in eternal lines to time thou grow'st.
     So long as men can breathe or eyes can see,
     So long lives this, and this gives life to thee.

(Shakespeare 1977: 19)

New Improved Sonnet XVIII by Peter Titheradge

Shall I equate thee with a summer's day?
Thou art more valid and more meaningful:
A north-west airstream will devalue May,
And summer's mortgage is forecloseable:
Sometimes the sun is too intensive-phased,
And often is his gold down-marketed,
And every fare by next year's fare's erased,
By an inflation situation fed:
But thy eternal summer's index-linked,
Nor shalt thou thine exclusive image lack,
Nor rate thy life-expectancy extinct,
When hopefully thou'rt out in paperback,
    So long as I'm in print and men are human,
    This is thy life-insurance, I'm thy Pru-man.

(Brett 1984: 311)

ACTIVITY 9:

Below is a passage taken from James Finn Garner's bestseller *Politically Correct Bedtime Stories: Modern Tales For Our Life and Times* (1994). In this book, Garner has rewritten a series of folktales by Hans Christian Anderson and the Brothers Grimm to remove any sexist, discriminatory or culturally biased elements – with some very funny results. Read through the following passages which are taken from the rewrite of 'Little Red Riding Hood' and consider how Garner has altered the story. Think about the conventions of folktales you have read. How has Garner altered the register from that of a traditional folktale? What specific word choices has he made? Would you call this a pastiche or parody? How is the humour created? If you are working in groups, discuss these questions together. Write up your points in a short report.

'Little Red Riding Hood'

There once was a young person named Red Riding Hood who lived with her mother on the edge of a large wood. One day her mother asked her to take a basket of fresh fruit and mineral water to her grandmother's house – not because this was woman's work, mind you, but because the deed was generous and helped engender a feeling of community. . . .

    On the way to Grandma's house, Red Riding Hood was accosted by a wolf. . . . The wolf said, 'You know, my dear, it isn't safe for a little girl to walk through these woods alone.'

    Red Riding Hood said, 'I find your sexist remark offensive in the extreme, but I will ignore it because of your traditional status as an outcast from society, the stress of which has caused you to develop your own, entirely valid, worldview.'

    Red Riding Hood walked on along the main path. But, because his status outside society had freed him from slavish adherence to linear, Western-style thought, the wolf knew a quicker route to Grandma's house. He burst into the house and ate Grandma . . . Then, unhampered by rigid, traditionalist notions of what was masculine or feminine, he put on Grandma's nightclothes and crawled into bed.

(Garner 1994: 1–3)

Garner's version follows the traditional pattern of the story with Red Riding Hood noting the enormous size of the wolf's eyes, nose and teeth, before being attacked. But when the woodcutter enters to save the day, Red Riding Hood turns on him:

'Bursting in here like a Neanderthal, trusting your weapon to do your thinking for you!' she exclaimed. 'Sexist! Speciesist! How dare you assume that women and wolves can't solve their own problems without a man's help!'

When she heard Red Riding Hood's impassioned speech, Grandma jumped out of the wolf's mouth, seized the woodchopper-person's axe, and cut his head off. After this ordeal, Red Riding Hood, Grandma, and the wolf felt a certain commonality of purpose. They decided to set up an alternative household based on mutual respect and cooperation, and they lived together in the woods happily ever after.

(Garner 1994: 4)

ACTIVITY 10:

Choose another literary text of about 300–500 words and write your own parody of it. Add a short commentary explaining how you went about the task and what you were trying to do with your parody or pastiche.

Alternatively, write a very short story (300–500 words) in which register is used to create comic effects. Write a short commentary on your story.

Summary

In this chapter we have examined:

- the importance of understanding context and audience for writing/ reading a text and making/hearing a speech act
- appropriate and inappropriate registers
- the effects of word choice and the relationship between word choice and register
- synonyms, connotations, collocations, open and closed word classes
- the use of discourse worlds
- the use and misuse of register in humour – pastiche, parody, malapropism.

References

Buczacki, Stefan (1994) *Best Shade Plants*. London: Reed.

Garner, James Finn (1994) *Politically Correct Bedtime Stories: Modern Tales For Our Life and Times*. New York: Macmillan.

Kafka, Franz (1978) *Metamorphosis and Other Stories*, trans. Willa and Edwin Muir. London: Penguin.

Salinger, J.D. (1951) *The Catcher in the Rye*. London: Little, Brown & Co.

Shakespeare, William (1977) *Shakespeare's Sonnets* [1564–1616]. London: Yale University Press.

CHAPTER 3

Writing in clear English

Simon Avery

I n the last chapter we examined the relations between style, audience and context in a variety of different types of writing. We looked at the importance of choosing an appropriate register and vocabulary when producing any particular piece of text, and paid attention to the idea of discourse worlds. In this chapter we're going to explore these ideas further by focusing on a number of styles of writing all of which we can incorporate under the term of clear English, where the emphasis lies on clarity, immediacy and accessibility. The main part of the chapter examines a range of strategies for improving the clarity of a number of public documents such as government leaflets and forms, business letters and legal writings – that is, texts which are read by a wide range of the public from different social and educational backgrounds. In the last sections, however, we will explore how some of these strategies can be used in academic writing, and how clear English has also been used by a number of literary writers from different historical periods and cultures.

We should emphasise here that writing in a clear English style (of which there are many) does not mean writing basic English or writing as if you are addressing a juvenile audience. Neither does it mean writing in a crude or unsophisticated style. Indeed, English can still be elegant, sophisticated and subtle when it is immediate and accessible. Of course, there will be situations where it is neither desirable nor necessary to write in clear English and where more difficult and demanding language styles will be more appropriate (we will look at some of these in the following chapter). As we emphasise throughout this book, you should always aim for a style which is suitable both for your audience and the context in which you are writing.

Clear English in the public sphere

Over the course of the twentieth century, many individuals and groups have called for the use of clear English in documents produced by the government, other public institutions and commerce. One of the most influential voices was that of the novelist and journalist George Orwell. In 1946 Orwell wrote an essay entitled 'Politics and the English Language', in which he argued that the English language was in a state of general collapse and decay. In particular, he attacked the writings and speeches of politicians, which he maintained were characterised by such a verbose and long-winded style that their meaning was often obscured rather than elucidated. Orwell's argument highlights the ways in which politicians used such a style to hide the real facts and implications of their political actions:

> A mass of Latin words falls upon the facts like soft snow, blurring the outlines and covering up all the details. The great enemy of clear language is insincerity. When there is a gap between one's real and one's declared aims, one turns as it were instinctively to long words and exhausted idioms, like a cuttlefish squirting ink.

(Orwell 1968: 363)

ACTIVITY 1:

Record an interview with a politician on the radio or television. Do you think Orwell's complaint is still relevant to today's politicians? Listen for words that you think are being used to avoid issues or to avoid being pinned down. Listen particularly for mechanical phrases such as 'at the end of the day' or 'the fact of the matter is'. Write a short report on the use of 'long words and exhausted idioms' in the interview you have studied.

Despite Orwell's pessimism about the contemporary state of the English language, he did believe that the process of deterioration could be reversed if only people were prepared to make a difference:

> Modern English, especially written English, is full of bad habits which spread by imitation and which can be avoided if one is willing to take the necessary trouble. If one gets rid of these habits one can think more clearly, and to think clearly is a necessary first step towards political regeneration: so that the fight against bad English is not frivolous and is not the exclusive concern of professional writers.

(Orwell 1968: 355)

Significantly, therefore, Orwell argues that his call for clear English is nothing less than an opportunity to bring about political and social change. This is an idea which certainly gained momentum as the twentieth century progressed. In 1950, for example, the British government commissioned Ernest Gowers to produce a document promoting the use of clear English in the civil service. The result of his work, *The Complete Plain Words*, is still in use today in revised editions, and, like Orwell's essay discussed above, it has informed the development of other campaigns for clear English in the sphere of public life.

Over the last twenty years the call for greater clarity in writings addressed to the public in Britain has largely been the result of the Plain English Campaign, founded in 1979. The Plain English Campaign was initially established in order to bring attention to the complexity of official government forms. Many forms produced by the civil service were so complicated and inaccessible that people who wanted to claim financial support, for example, could not understand them and were therefore losing out. Other public institutions were equally unskilled in conveying information, and consequently the general public had become used to associating bureaucracy with incomprehensible language, jargon and legalese. The letter below, written to a tenant of a council-owned property, is an example of the type of document which the Plain English Campaign have been trying to change:

Dear Sir/Madam,

I am writing to inform you that the City Council at their meeting on 25th July, 1979, in accordance with the duty imposed by Section 113 (1A) of the Housing Act, 1957, to review rents from time to time and to make such changes, either of the rents generally or of particular rents, as circumstances may require, decided that the net rents (i.e. exclusive of rates) of all Council-owned dwellings should continue to be related to Gross Rateable Values and adopted a general basis of 130% of Gross Rateable Value as the level at which the net rents should be set.

New rents are at present based on 100% of Gross Rateable Values and, as a first step towards achieving the new basis of assessment, the Council have decided that those rents which are below 130% of Gross Rateable Value should be increased with effect from the rent week beginning Monday, 1st October, 1979, by 60p per week, or by such appropriate lesser amount as is required to bring them up to the level of 130% of Gross Value, and that current rents which are in excess of 130% Gross Value should remain unchanged.

(Plain English Campaign 1993: 10)

As you'll probably agree, such writing is hard to decipher and the reader might have to read it several times to understand it.

As the Plain English Campaign and others like it (the Better English Campaign and the Plain Language Action Network, for example) tend to focus specifically on documents within the public sphere, they have always had a very strong political dimension (connecting, therefore, to Orwell's ideas above). From its outset, for example, the Plain English Campaign made its presence felt through a series of public demonstrations against official writings, including shredding hundreds of government forms in London's Parliament Square. Within three years of being founded, however, the Campaign had become so prominent that the Conservative government under Margaret Thatcher used it as an adviser to the Cabinet. One major result of this collaboration was the issuing of a White Paper in 1982 which asked all government departments to improve the accessibility and clarity of any forms which the public were asked to complete. Bureaucratese and legalese therefore started to come under sustained attack through official channels. (You can find out more about the Plain English Campaign in *The Plain English Story*, 1993.)

Britain has not been the only country to benefit from campaigns calling for clearer English. In 1998 the American president Bill Clinton made writing in clear English a priority for his administration, as this extract from the official White House memorandum reveals:

The White House
June 1, 1998
Memorandum for the heads of executive departments and agencies
Subject: Plain Language in Government Writing

The Vice President and I have made reinventing the Federal Government a top priority of my Administration. We are determined to make the Government more responsive, accessible, and understandable in its communications with the public.

The Federal Government's writing must be in plain language. By using plain language, we send a clear message about what the Government is doing, what it requires, and what services it offers. Plain language saves the Government and the private sector time, effort, and money.

Plain language requirements vary from one document to another, depending on the intended audience. Plain language documents have logical organization, easy-to-read design features, and use:

- common, everyday words, except for necessary technical terms;
- 'you' and other pronouns;
- the active voice; and
- short sentences.

(http://www.plainlanguage.gov)

We'll return to these elements of a clear English style below. For the moment, though, it is important to emphasise the major role which governments believe such writing takes in the modern world. Indeed, the Plain English Campaign has even worked with South Africa's Ministry of Justice to redraft the 1995 Human Rights Commission Act into clear English (Plain English Campaign 1996: 1). Making information accessible and comprehensible is therefore considered an essential part of the process of empowering people and encouraging greater democracy.

Government departments are not the only institutions which have realised the benefits of using a clear English style. Many businesses and commercial institutions, for example, have discovered how producing documents in clearer English can improve relations with their customers. Writing in a clear, precise and accessible style certainly seems to be a major asset for companies seeking to market their products effectively and win customers.

The work of organisations such as the Plain English Campaign is therefore anti-bureaucratic, fighting against pomposity, wordiness, jargon, and the lack of any consideration of audience. In promoting a style which is clear, crisp and well-organised, they seek to encourage writers in the public sphere to elucidate rather than conceal their thought, and to produce documents which empower rather than oppress the reader.

Writing in a clear English style

Clear writers, like clear fountains, do not seem so deep as they are; the turbid look the most profound.

(Walter Savage Landor, *Imaginary Conversations*, 1824)

In this section we are going to introduce you to some of the main techniques of writing in a clear English style, showing you how your writing can be made more lucid and accessible for your readers. We should stress here, however, that these are not prescriptive rules – you will need to decide whether they are appropriate for the piece of work you are producing and the audience you are addressing. And, of course, we are not proposing that you get rid of your personal style – we all have individual approaches when we write and this is important for variety and originality. Rather, the suggestions below will help you communicate your ideas with clarity, skill and precision. Remember, clearer writing can often be more stimulating and interesting for your readers as they won't be required to wade through a quagmire of verbiage and serpentine syntax – and good, accessible, appropriate communication is what this book is all about.

The following points, drawn in part from the work of Orwell, Gowers and the Plain English Campaign, are widely accepted as the core ideas of writing in a clear English style.

Choose suitable words

Words, like glass, obscure when they do not aid vision.

(Joseph Joubert, *Pensées*, 1842)

Word choice is one of the most important elements in making sure that writing is clear, immediate and accessible to the reader. Sometimes, however, a piece of prose reads as if the author has purposely gone out of his/her way to include as many long and unfamiliar words as possible. You might have come across pieces like this yourself. Often writers of such confusing pieces use complex words in the mistaken belief that this will make them sound impressive and powerful. Possibly even worse is the use of long words merely to hide an absence of ideas: the writer has little to say and therefore attempts to mask this through complicated language. Whatever the reasons, little consideration is paid to the audience by the writer in these circumstances, and there is a real danger that the piece of writing will not achieve its aims because readers can't understand it. There's also the danger, of course, that readers won't even bother to finish the piece because they might not have the patience or willingness to keep looking up unfamiliar or obscure words in the dictionary.

To avoid this situation, you should be extremely careful in your choice of diction. Avoid awkward, polysyllabic words which might be alien to your audience. English is an incredibly rich and versatile language with more words than many other languages (more than twice as many as French, for example), which means that you should easily be able to find an alternative for any word which might be unfamiliar to your audience. Very often, using more familiar words will make the meaning of your writing more punchy, since it will be more readily understood and recalled later. And after all, writing in a clear English style should be about good communication, not translation!

ACTIVITY 2:

Bearing the above points about word choice in mind, look at the following list of words, all of which are commonly used in public documents. The first half are English and the second half are Latin abbreviations and foreign words. How many do you recognise? Can you think of alternatives for them? If you are working in a study group, discuss your suggestions with the other group members. Once you have completed the exercise, consider if you find all of these words problematic. Are there any which you feel would be suitable for inclusion in a public document?

English words (v = verb, adv = adverb, n = noun, adj = adjective)
accede to (v)
acquiesce (v)
aggregate (v)
alleviate (v)
ameliorate (v)
apprise (v)
axiomatic (adj)
behove (v)
cognisant (adj)
contingent upon (adj)
domiciled in (v)
erroneous (adj)
eventuate (v)
evince (v)
exigency (n)
expedite (v)
extant (adj)
hold in abeyance (v)
mandatory (adj)
promulgate (v)
pursuant (adv)

Latin abbreviations and foreign words
ad hoc
carte blanche
et al. (et alia)
ex officio
ibid. (ibidem)
inter alia
modus operandi
per capita
pro rata
per se
viz. (videlicet)

Avoid inappropriate use of jargon

This is another thorny issue where word choice is concerned. The *Oxford English Dictionary* defines jargon in the following ways:

1. the specialised vocabulary of a particular trade, profession, group or activity.
2. *derog[atory]* language which uses this type of vocabulary in a pretentious or meaningless way.
3. confusing or meaningless talk; gibberish.

These three definitions reflect the main attitudes towards jargon. As a specialised vocabulary, it is acceptable to use jargon if you are addressing somebody in the same profession or group (what we have previously called a 'discourse world' – see Chapter 2). But when we are addressing somebody outside that group, jargon should be avoided if it is likely to be confusing. In some professions, such as the legal profession, it is evident that jargon is often used to keep the layperson in the dark and to act as a means of exclusion (see below for further exploration of legal writing). Similarly, the world of management theory has developed its own scientific-sounding jargon over the last decade, often, it seems, to exclude those who are not 'in the know'. Words such as 'outplacement', 'downsizing' and 'delayering' have little currency outside management circles (the first two are euphemisms for redundancy and the last means getting rid of management hierarchies), while some terms seem to be invented simply in order to give the most mundane of tasks a certain grandeur. We recently heard, for example, of the case of a manager being invited to engage in 'flipchart information capture' at a conference – an over-elaborate phrase for simply writing his answers to various questions on the board! Below is a sentence which, although invented by us, is typical of this kind of 'management-speak'. How would you translate it?

We sincerely believe that the employment of elucidated and rationalised aims and objectives will optimise our capacity for prioritising our energies so that they will impact more efficiently and intensely upon the major thrust of our institution's future plans and prospects.

Be aware of overly long sentences

I am quite capable of speaking, unprepared, a sentence containing anything up to forty subordinate clauses all embedded in their neighbours like those wooden Russian dolls, and many a native of these islands, speaking English as to the manner born, has followed me trustingly into the labyrinth only to perish miserably trying to find the way out.

(Bernard Levin, *In These Times*, 1986)

Avoiding overly long sentences is one of the most important guidelines of writing in a clear English style. As Levin suggests above, it is quite easy to create sentences which seem to go on and on and on, stretching endlessly down the page, packed with clause upon clause, so that the whole gets longer and longer and the reader ends up either forgetting the main point of the piece of writing or falling asleep or both. See what we mean?

Of course, long sentences can sometimes be necessary and valuable (can you think of any examples from your own experience?), but if they're not carefully controlled there's a danger of your writing becoming confusing for both you and your readers. Overly complex syntax can end up masking more information than it reveals and might also suggest to your readers that your own thought processes are confused and badly developed. So aim for precision and clarity in your writing, and use straightforward word order wherever possible. There's often no need to write complex sentences to make an impact, as many professional writers (journalists, novelists, advertisers and critics) have demonstrated.

ACTIVITY 3:

Below are two overly long sentences. Consider where you might break them up so that the overall sense is easier to follow. If you are working in a group, discuss your decisions with the other group members. In what different ways could you split the sentences?

> Having met with the management team in the marketing department of our sister company and having discussed with them your proposal for marketing the new product, to be produced by your own company, with them and considered its potential place in relation to our own products and the possibilities of advertising it both through our existing catalogue and various other outlets, it has been agreed that it would be extremely premature to give you a definite answer at the present moment since the research and development is only at an early stage and extensive testing will have to be undertaken before the final approval can be given.

> I refer to your recent letter regarding the irregularity of your hire purchase repayments, but as you are now several months behind on your repayment, despite the opportunities granted you by ourselves to renegotiate an alternative plan of monthly instalments and interest rate, I have no other course of action open to me but to proceed with court action and therefore details of your account have now been forwarded to our solicitor who will no doubt be contacting you in due course with regard to the matter.

Tackling wordiness and improving conciseness

If there is anywhere a thing said in two sentences that could have been as clearly and as engagingly said in one, then it's amateur work.

(Robert Louis Stevenson, letter of 1888)

A particular problem for many writers is the tendency to pad out their writing with words which aren't needed and which add nothing to the overall sense. If you feel you suffer from this, don't worry, as everyone does at times. The trick is to be prepared to edit your work ruthlessly, prune any words or phrases which are not essential, and aim for concise sentences where every word serves a purpose and works for its space. Although this process will take time, the result will be that your writing is sharper, clearer and more precise.

A good place to start when aiming for conciseness and compression in your writing is to think about what your readers already know, what they don't need to know, and what they will be able to infer. There will then often be no need to include these details and you'll already be saving yourself both space and time. Another important area that you should pay attention to is the use of what we can call 'filler words', which can be divided into four main groups:

- Words relating to categories. For example, some writers have a tendency to write phrases such as 'small in size' or 'in a distressed state' rather than simply 'small' or 'distressed'. The other words are simply fillers and can be taken out. Similar phrases include 'light in weight', 'of an expensive quality' and 'of an odd type'.
- Words which state the obvious. For example, 'She is a woman who likes reading' can be simply rewritten as 'She likes reading' – the rest of the information is obvious.
- Modifiers such as 'really', 'basically', 'actually', 'kind of', 'sort of', which add nothing in most cases and can therefore be easily removed.
- Redundant pairs of words. Many words imply each other so there is no need to use both. Consider, for example, the phrases 'free gift', 'future plans', 'end result', 'unexpected surprise', 'past memories', 'true facts'. In each of these cases, the phrase can be reduced to one word and mean the same. Can you think of other examples?

A final point in this section concerns the use of excessive detail. It is a common tendency for writers to pack their work full of details which can then make the piece hard to read and follow. Chekhov, the Russian playwright, drew attention to this in a letter written in 1899:

If I write, 'A man sat down on the grass', it is understandable because it is clear and doesn't require a second reading. But it would be hard to follow and brain-taxing were I to write, 'A tall, narrow-chested, red-bearded man of medium height sat down noiselessly, looking around timidly and in fright, on a patch of green grass that had once been trampled by pedestrians.'

(Quoted in Kemp 1997: 235)

Although Chekhov is obviously overstating his point here, he clearly shows the dangers of excessive detail. So always be ready to go back over your work and think carefully about each word and phrase. If you find yourself repeating your points, adding unnecessary words or writing with excessive detail, make sure you edit the piece carefully so that the essential meaning is brought nearer to the surface and the whole is more precise and exact. (We will look in more detail at strategies for effective editing in the following chapter, 'From draft to draft'.)

ACTIVITY 4:

Look at the following letter written to a student who wants to attend a conference on the poets of the Romantic period. How would you improve it and make it more concise? Think carefully about where the writer is being repetitive and what could be cut without losing the essential points. For example, in the first sentence it is unnecessary to write both 'yesterday morning' and the date, and the whole second sentence could be rephrased to get rid of the clumsy sounding 'The question as to whether...'. Make cuts and changes where you think necessary, then redraft the whole piece so that it flows well. Add a commentary giving reasons for your changes.

I am writing this letter to inform you that, following your telephone conversation to myself yesterday morning at 10.25 a.m. on Wednesday 22nd July 1998, I take the greatest pleasure in sending you details and information of the forthcoming conference 'Visions and Revisions: Romantic Poetry in the New Millennium' to be held on Saturday next weekend. The question as to whether we will be able to furnish you with car parking space for your vehicle on the particular day in question is still unresolved. In connection with this, you would be advised to communicate your requirements directly to the supervising attendant on duty on your immediate arrival. Owing to the fact that space assigned to the parking of cars on the premises is severely limited, it might be pertinent for you to consider leaving your vehicle at another carpark in the vicinity near to the university.

The morning's activities will be constituted of a series of lectures which will be informative in nature and which will permit a variety of issues to be raised and addressed. The keynote talk will be orchestrated by Dr James MacDonald, Ph.D., a man who is widely recognised across the world as a knowledgeable authority in his specific discipline area. In the afternoon the delegates will participate in a series of mini workshops which will be small in size where they will engage in debate concerning the ideas explored in the lectures given during the morning. We hope the day will be a highly interesting and engaging one for you and we look forward with pleasure to welcoming you for our conference next Saturday.

In the event of the conference having to be cancelled on the particular day in question due to any unforeseen circumstance, we will do our utmost to effect the reimbursement of the monies due to any particular delegate.

Use active rather than passive verbs

Verbs can be divided into two groups, active and passive, which produce very different effects in a piece of writing. So what is the difference between the two groups?

Consider this simple sentence:

> The teacher dropped the pile of books.

Here the subject is 'the teacher' (the agent or doer of the action), the verb is 'dropped', and the object is 'the pile of books'. Sentences written in the active voice always follow this grammatical pattern: subject – verb – object (although they do not always need to have an object). It is therefore clear who is performing the action of the verb.

In sentences written in the passive voice, however, the order is reversed. Rather than the subject performing the action of the verb, the subject is acted upon. If we rewrite the above sentence in the passive, for example, it would become:

Passive subject	Verb	Agent
The pile of books	was dropped	by the teacher.

A passive construction can always be identified by its use of

- the verb 'to be' in some form (is, are, was, were, will be, been, being, etc.)
- a past participle (for example, shut, dropped, demanded, thought).

(Can you spot the passive construction which has been used in this sentence?)

One of the main results of passive constructions is that the 'doer' of the action is either left until the end of the sentence or omitted altogether. For instance, in the example above, we only find who dropped the books at the end of the sentence. This has the effect of making the sentence less dramatic and not as forceful as the active sentence. Compare the following, for example:

> Active: She slammed the brakes on as the car sped downhill.
> Passive: The brakes of the car were slammed on by the driver as the car sped downhill.

Both these sentences refer to the same action, but the first is more dramatic as it is shorter and less convoluted.

In other passive constructions the agent is missed out completely so that the sentence appears completely impersonal. For example, in the sentence 'Assignments will be distributed next week', we are not told who will do the distributing. Similarly, in the sentence 'The computer monitor was smashed and thrown on the floor', we are not told who did the damage. This type of passive construction is often used to avoid allocating blame or taking responsibility for something, as in the sentence 'Next week the factory will be closed and four hundred employees will be made redundant'.

If you want your prose to be clear and direct, you should try to use active sentences as often as possible. They are usually easier to read, sound crisper and keep the human agent visible. To change a passive sentence into an active sentence, simply identify the agent/doer of the action and make it the subject:

Passive: *Jane Eyre* was considered to be a revolutionary book by many Victorian readers.

Active: Many Victorian readers considered *Jane Eyre* to be a revolutionary book.

Extra note on passives

There are, however, several occasions when the passive voice can be useful or appropriate or necessary:

- When you want to avoid being accusatory. For example, 'Unfortunately the appointment was not kept' is more polite than the blunter 'You did not keep your appointment'.
- When you want to avoid showing direct responsibility, as in the example of the factory closure above. Another example would be the use of 'Bagdad was bombed last night' rather than 'American bombers bombed Bagdad last night'.
- When writing scientific reports where the use of the passive is the usual convention. For example, 'The test tube of fluid was heated over a medium flame and changes in its colour were recorded'.
- When you want to emphasise what is happening more than who is doing it. For example: 'Last night a young girl was brutally murdered in Camden', 'The kidney transplant was considered a great success', or 'The Romantic poets are primarily revered for their revival of the ballad form'.

Again, when making the decision whether to use active or passive constructions, you will have to consider which is most suitable for both your audience and the context of the piece you are writing.

Use verbs instead of nominalisations

A nominalisation is the name given to a noun when it is formed from a verb. For example, 'investigation' is the nominalisation of the verb 'to investigate' and 'production' is the nominalisation of the verb 'to produce'. What are the nominalisations of the verbs to analyse, to assess, to manage, to present?

In most circumstances it is better to use the verb form when you write rather than an abstract nominalisation, as the verb has the effect of making your writing sound more active and dynamic. As an example, consider the following sentence:

> Yesterday we held a discussion concerning the future restructuring of Impact Incorporated and we reached a decision that, as a first initiative, all costs will have to be cut back as far as possible.

Here there are two nominalisations ('discussion' and 'decision') which can be put back into the verb form:

> Yesterday we discussed the future restructuring of Impact Incorporated and decided that, as a first initiative, all costs will have to be cut back as far as possible.

Already, the sentence sounds more active and energetic. (Bearing in mind the other guidelines for improving clarity and conciseness we have looked at, is there anything else in this sentence you could change?) We are not saying, of course, that there is no place for nominalisations or abstract nouns (they are often needed in scientific or academic writing, for example), but you should try to avoid them as far as possible if you are aiming for clarity and immediacy. How might you rewrite the following sentences?

> The Vice Chancellor conducted an investigation into the matter in a swift manner. Attempts were made on the part of the management team with regard to an assessment and revaluation of the project.

Use positive statements wherever possible

Negative constructions can often be confusing as readers have to 'translate' the negatives into positives in order to find out what they can or should do. For example, the sentence

> If you do not sign the enclosed payment form, then we will not be able to process your order.

has to be mentally 'translated' into:

> Please sign the enclosed payment form so we can process your order.

Similarly, the sentence

> Fewer marks are given to those essays which lack a proper bibliography.

needs to be translated into:

> We will give a higher mark to an essay which has a proper bibliography.

In both cases, the positive version is clearer, more polite and saves on words. You'll also notice that in the revised version of the second sentence we get rid of a passive construction as well.

Use language which is gender-neutral and non-discriminatory

Over the last few decades the use of language which is seen as discriminatory against any group has become unacceptable to many people. This includes language which discriminates on the grounds of gender, sexual orientation, religion, nationality, age, or socio-economic background. Most house styles used in the workplace require writers to use language which is free from discrimination, either explicitly or implicitly, so it is particularly important that you think carefully about your words and phrases with this in mind. Try to avoid gender-specific terms such as 'salesgirl' or 'sculptress', for example, where the suffix might be seen to trivialise women. It is also important to be wary of the use of 'man' as a collective noun since it again implies that women are secondary. There are many non-sexist alternatives which can be used instead.

ACTIVITY 5:

Think of non-sexist alternatives for the following terms. Can you think of any other terms which might be problematic?

mankind
man-made
the man in the street
a number of man-hours
chairman

Another area of contention is the use of pronouns. English does not have a pronoun which can be used to refer to both sexes so there is a tendency to use 'he', 'his' and 'him' to cover both male and female, as in the sentence 'Every student should hand in his essay before the end of the week'. However, there are several alternatives which can be used to avoid such gender bias:

- Replace the masculine pronoun with 'one', 'you' or 's/he'.
- Use the plural form – recently it has become more common to go against strict grammatical rules and use 'they', 'them' and 'their' as singulars. For example: 'Under the University's regulations each student must fill in the correct form before they can be formally registered on their course'.
- Rewrite the sentence in the plural to avoid the need for a singular pronoun. For example, 'Each student must hand in his assignment before Friday' can be rewritten as 'All students must hand in their assignments before Friday'.

Use a clear layout

In the sections above, we have indicated some of the main ways in which you can make your writing clearer, more accessible and more precise. Another major element in helping your readers to follow the content of your piece is the way it is laid out. In general, the presentation of your piece should display the information in a way which is easy to read, highlights the main points, and is visually appealing. This is obviously an extremely large area for consideration, but below are some pointers which you might want to bear in mind:

- Always aim to display your material in a clear and accessible manner – think of your readers and how they will be attracted to your work. If you are using diagrams or pictures, for example, think how they relate to the text. You might also want to consider the use of typographical features such as italics or underlining (see Chapter 6 for more on the use of these features in journalistic writing).

- Use plenty of white space so your reader is not bombarded with text. Putting white space around the text – margins or free lines – gives the eye somewhere to rest and therefore makes the reading experience easier.
- Use lists to present information. This breaks the information up so it can be more easily taken in. Using bullet points as in this list is a good idea, for example.

ACTIVITY 6:

Find a document which conveys information to the public and analyse how the layout is used to help convey that information. You might like to choose a leaflet from your local library or post office, for example, a section from a university prospectus or a government form.

To summarise

- The golden rule – as in all writing – is remember your readers. What is their background? What are they used to reading? What do you want them to gain from your piece? Imagine yourself as the reader of the text – where would the problem areas be?
- Think carefully about your diction. Are you using too many technical words? Will your readers understand the jargon which you take for granted? Overall, avoid any woolly phrases by making sure every word is clear and accurate. Try using a thesaurus so that your words are the most precise ones you can find (see Chapter 2 for more on synonyms).
- Avoid overly long sentences – split them if necessary.
- Cut excess verbiage – make every word count and don't overload your readers.
- Use active rather than passive verbs wherever possible.
- Use verbs rather than nominalisations.
- Use non-sexist and non-discriminatory language.
- Be prepared to edit and rework your writing so that the meaning is clear, crisp and concise. Editing helps clarify your ideas, your purpose in writing, and how your material can be shaped to best effect (see Chapter 4 on drafting). As Thornton Wilder once said in the *New York Times* (6 November 1961), a writer's best friend at this stage can often be the incinerator!

ACTIVITY 7:

Below are two business letters which are written in anything but clear English. Choose one of them and rewrite it to improve its style and accessibility. Include a commentary on what you decided to change and why.

To all managers,

Re: New London Telephone Numbers

You will no doubt have realised from the extensive national publicity on television and in the national newspapers concerning new London dialling codes that the prefix '01' for London which is in operation presently will cease to be available from the 6 of May this year.

On and following that specific date, old '01' numbers will be intercepted by BT equipment, and the expectation is that the gross congestion which will follow is likely to present severe delays in reaching the London area (in which over 40 per cent of all the telephones in the Kingdom are located).

In order not to compromise our normal business routine, I have arranged for the new codes (071 and 081) to be available to us from next Tuesday 17 April. Please inform all the staff that you have responsibility and control for that as from that date:

(a) '01' numbers cannot be dialled from the company's telephonic systems;
(b) should a member of staff incorrectly dial '071' instead of '081' as the prefix to a London number, a recorded announcement will announce the correct code for the numbers misdialled.

I very much hope that this advance programme of adaptation will assist us in being able without difficulty to continue after the 6 of May to function as efficiently as before.

To whom it may concern,

Re: Parking in George Street

It has recently been drawn to my attention that non-authorised motor vehicles have been parked regularly and for long duration in the car park adjoining George Street.

If these vehicles are connected with your business, I should be obliged if you would cease this practice immediately and forthwith as the trespass of motor vehicles on the leasehold property of AA Jones and Sons is an offence under the Common Law of this country.

Should parking on the aforementioned said car park persist I must inform you that the local authorities will be notified without delay and the vehicles in question will be removed and the owner/s of the vehicles held responsible for the costs of removal and recovery.

It is possible that the offending vehicles are in the ownership of someone other than yourselves and if this is the case in this instance I would be exceedingly grateful if you would let me know so that I can take the necessary action to locate the owners.

Legal writing

One area which is still particularly resistant to the use of a clear English style is the law. For hundreds of years legal writing has been characterised by its inaccessibility, often being full of convoluted sentences, passive verb forms, terms borrowed from Latin and French, and archaic expressions such as 'heretofore', 'aforementioned', 'herein', 'aforesaid' and 'witnesseth'. (The way in which many of these terms are also used in more formal letters can be seen in the second letter of Activity 7 above.) This style has acquired such a tradition over the centuries that many lawyers now believe that complex legal documents cannot be expressed in any other way. There is no doubt, of course, that legal language has to be precise and accurate so that loopholes in the law are avoided, but in many cases, legal documents often seem to be unnecessarily complicated. Much of the energy of clear English groups is therefore now being directed into tackling these types of documents, showing that they don't need to be mystifying but can be written in clear English without losing the required precision (you might like to look, for example, at the website of Clarity, the world-wide lawyers' group campaigning for clearer English at http://www.adler.demon.co.uk/clarity.htm).

ACTIVITY 8:

Look at the following document. How would you redraft it so it can be clearly understood?

The undersigned Sarah Smith the mother and legal guardian of JOHN SMITH, of 5 Ambrose Street, Oxford, hereby solemnly and sincerely declare as follows: On behalf of the said JOHN SMITH I wholly renounce, relinquish, and abandon the use of his former surname of SMITH and on his behalf do assume from the date hereof the surname of JONES so that he may thereafter by called, known, and distinguished not by his former name of JOHN SMITH but by his assumed name of JOHN JONES. The said JOHN SMITH will at all times hereafter in all records, deed documents and other writings and in all actions and proceedings as well as in dealings and transactions and on all occasions whatsoever, use and subscribe the said name of JONES as his surname in substitution for his former surname of SMITH so relinquished as aforesaid to the intent that the said JOHN SMITH may hereafter be called, known, or distinguished not by the former surname of SMITH but by the surname of JONES only.

I on behalf of the said JOHN SMITH authorise and request all persons at all times hereafter to designate and address him by the adopted surname of JONES accordingly. I make this declaration believing the same to be true by virtue of the Statutory Declarations Act 1885, Signed

Postscript on legal language

Recently, various attempts have been made by members of the legal profession itself to bring about the use of clearer English. The most important movement so far is Lord Irvine's reforms of the civil legal system in April 1998, which ruled that Latin and legal jargon are barred from civil courts in England and Wales. This is a great step forward to introducing a clearer English style throughout the legal system, but there is still a long way to go.

ACTIVITY 9:

Since 1990 the Plain English Campaign has awarded a seal of approval called the Crystal Mark to documents which achieve a high degree of clarity. It has been awarded to many institutions in Britain and abroad, including the National Westminster Bank, British Telecom, Royal Mail and General Accident. Go to your local branch of the National Westminster Bank or one of these other companies and find one of their leaflets which has the Crystal Mark on it. You could ask one of the staff there to give their opinion of the Crystal Mark and the documents they use which have earned it. Then analyse the language of the leaflet either on your own or in your study group. What elements of a clear English style are evident in it? Is there anything you would want to change? Why do you think the leaflet qualifies for the Crystal Mark?

Clear English in academic work

Many of the points that we have examined above on writing clear, well-organised and accessible prose also apply to writing more academic pieces such as the essays you will be asked to produce if you are on a degree course. In writing an essay or piece of coursework, you will need to demonstrate not only that you have a sound understanding of your subject, but also that you are able to express your points with lucidity. Many essays at higher education level have a maximum word limit so you will have to be concise in your writing as well. If we look again at Orwell's essay 'Politics and the English Language', it is clear that he recognised the importance of clear English in academic writing just as much as in other forms of writing. Here, for example, he quotes from a scholarly essay on the poet John Milton in order to demonstrate how not to go about making an academic argument. See what you can make of it.

> I am not indeed sure whether it is not true to say that the Milton who once seemed not unlike a seventeenth-century Shelley had not become, out of an experience ever more bitter in each year, more alien to the founder of that Jesuit sect which nothing could induce him to tolerate.

(Quoted in Orwell 1968: 355)

This is certainly as confusing as many of the other documents we have been looking at. Have you come across examples of such inaccessible academic language yourself? Do you think there is a place for such writing at all?

Book 4 of this series, *Making Your Case: A Practical Guide to Essay Writing*, shows in detail a range of strategies for making sure your academic work is clear, accessible and effective. For the present, though, it is useful to draw attention to the way in which many of the techniques described in this chapter can help you to do this too.

ACTIVITY 10:

Below is a passage taken from the opening of Francis Wheen's biography of Karl Marx. Read it through and then analyse how effective you think it is. Consider clarity, word choice, sentence structure, the use of active or passive verb forms, and how the material is organised. In what ways is this piece different from the piece above which Orwell criticised? Do you think this is a good piece of academic writing? Is there anything you would like to change? Are there any techniques used here which you feel you could use in your own essays?

There were only eleven mourners at Karl Marx's funeral on 17 March 1883. 'His name and work will endure through the ages,' Friedrich Engels predicted in a graveside oration at Highgate cemetery. It seemed an unlikely boast, but he was right.

The history of the twentieth century is Marx's legacy. Stalin, Mao, Che, Castro – the icons and monsters of the modern age have all presented themselves as his heirs. Whether he would recognise them as such is quite another matter. Even in his lifetime, the antics of self-styled disciples often drove him to despair. On hearing that a new French party claimed to be Marxist, he replied that in that case 'I, at least, am not a Marxist'. Nevertheless, within one hundred years of his death half the world's population was ruled by governments that professed Marxism to be their guiding faith. His ideas have transformed the study of economics, history, geography, sociology and literature. Not since Jesus Christ has an obscure pauper inspired such global devotion – or been so calamitously misinterpreted.

(Wheen 1999: 1)

Clear English in Literature

Literature is often celebrated for its ambiguity, complexity and richness of language, but there is also a strong tradition of literature written in clear English which stretches back to seventeenth-century Protestant writings. Authors as varied as Francis Bacon and Ernest Hemingway, Jonathan Swift and Toni Morrison, Anthony Trollope and Kurt Vonnegut often use the techniques for clear writing which we have outlined in this chapter. Here, for example, is a passage from Daniel Defoe's famous novel *Robinson Crusoe* (1719) when the protagonist is on board a ship during a violent storm:

> We had a good Ship, but she was deep loaden, and wallowed in the Sea, that the Seamen every now and then cried out, she would founder. It was my Advantage in one respect, that I did not know what they meant by Founder, till I enquir'd. However, the Storm was so violent, that I saw what is not often seen, the Master, the Boat-Swain, and some others more sensible than the rest, at their Prayers, and expecting every Moment that the Ship would go to the Bottom. In the Middle of the Night, and under all the rest of our Distresses, one of the Men that had been down on Purpose to see, cried out we had sprung a Leak; another said there was four Foot Water in the Hold. Then all hands were called to the Pump. At that very Word my Heart, as I thought, died within me, and I fell backwards upon the Side of my Bed where I sat, into the Cabbin. However, the Men roused me, and told me, that I that was able to do nothing before, was as well able to pump as another; at which I stirr'd up, and went to the Pump and work'd very heartily.

(Defoe 1975: 12)

Defoe is often regarded as the father of journalism, a form of writing which promotes clarity and accessibility (see Chapter 6), and there is certainly something of the dramatic journalistic narrative about this piece. He directly represents the urgent situation as the sailors struggle to stop the ship from sinking, through a plain, strong and vigorous style. Overall the diction is extremely precise and effective; throughout Defoe uses active verb forms which, as we have discussed above, keep the human agents visible and reinforce the sense of action. There is little use of modifiers or filler words, and the author has clearly thought carefully about word choice. The description of the ship 'wallow[ing]' in the sea, for example, gives us a good sense of the weight on board and the vessel's struggle through the ocean. The author also uses syntax and sentence length to help represent the men battling with the storm. The end of the fourth sentence, for example, builds up details of the ship's disintegration through the effective use of the semi-colon ('one of the Men . . . cried out we had sprung a Leak; another said there was four Foot Water in the hold'), while the brevity of the following sentence ('Then all hands were called to the Pump') emphasises the urgency of the situation and the need for everyone to help. Throughout the piece, the focus lies firmly on describing the action concisely and vividly, in a way which certainly reveals Defoe's commitment to writing in a clear English style. What other techniques or elements of language do you notice in this passage which help to contribute to the effect?

ACTIVITY 11:

Read the passage below taken from the opening of Toni Morrison's *Sula*, a novel about American racial injustice set in Medallion, a small town where the black population has been repeatedly marginalised by the whites. Analyse the piece in detail and consider which elements of a clear English style are being used here. If you feel there are aspects of the passage which can't be described in terms of a clear English style, note those down too. Then write up your analysis in the form of a short report. Once you have completed your report, consider what differences, if any, you think there are between the use of a clear English style in a public document and the use of a clear English style in a piece of literature.

> In that place, where they tore the nightshade and blackberry patches from their roots to make room for the Medallion City Golf Course, there was once a neighbourhood. It stood in the hills above the valley town of Medallion and spread all the way to the river. It is called the suburbs now, but when black people lived there it was called the Bottom. One road, shaded by beeches, oaks, maples and chestnuts, connected it to the valley. The beeches are gone now, and so are the pear trees where children sat and yelled down through the blossoms to passers by. Generous funds have been allotted to level the stripped and faded buildings that clutter the road from Medallion up to the golf course. They are going to raze the Time and a Half Pool hall, where feet in long tan shoes once pointed down from chair rungs. A steel ball will knock to dust Irene's Palace of Cosmetology, where women used to lean their heads back on sink trays and doze while Irene lathered Nu Nile into their hair. Men in Khaki work clothes will pry loose the slats of Reba's Grill, where the owner cooked in her hat because she couldn't remember the ingredients without it.
>
> (Morrison 1982: 11)

ACTIVITY 12:

Choose a passage of about 150 words by an author who, in your opinion, writes in a clear English style. Analyse the passage in detail and make a list of the specific techniques which are used. Then write a passage of your own on the same or a different subject in the style of the author you have chosen.

Summary

In this chapter we have looked at:

- the use of a clear English style in a range of public documents
- a number of strategies for improving clarity and accessibility when writing

- how clear English can be used in academic writing
- how clear English can be used by authors of literary works.

References

Defoe, Daniel (1975) *Robinson Crusoe*. New York: W.W. Norton.
Gowers, Ernest (1986) *The Complete Plain Words*. London: HMSO.
Kemp, Peter (1997) *The Oxford Dictionary of Literary Quotations*. Oxford: Oxford University Press.
Morrison, Toni (1982) *Sula*. London: Grafton Books.
Orwell, George (1968) *Essays*. Harmondsworth: Penguin.
Plain English Campaign (1993) *The Plain English Story*. Stockport: Plain English Campaign.
Plain English Campaign (1996) *Campaign International*. Stockport: Plain English Campaign.
Wheen, Francis (1999) *Karl Marx*. London: Fourth Estate.

From draft to draft: refreshing words

Rebecca Stott

n the last chapter we considered ways of keeping prose absolutely clear. In its efforts to make writing accessible, the Plain English Campaign tends to emphasise short sentences and simple grammatical structures, but there is much writing that retains clarity while placing greater demands on the reader in terms of vocabulary and complex grammatical structures. Once again, context and purpose are important considerations here. Some ideas – in academic, analytical or philosophical writing, for instance – need to be expressed in complex and demanding ways. The novelist Henry James, renowned for his convoluted prose style, once claimed in an essay called 'The Art of Fiction' (1884) that:

> Experience is never limited, and it is never complete; it is an immense sensibility, a kind of huge spider-web of the finest silken threads suspended in the chamber of consciousness, and catching every air-borne particle in its tissue.

(James 1957: 23)

Henry James's prose style is as complex and intricate as a spider-web, then, partly because of his attempt to express the 'immense sensibility' of human experience.

In this chapter our focus will not be so much on clarity and simplicity of style but rather on the question of how to ensure that what we write – whether it is plain, complex or ornate in style – is fresh, interesting and lively through editing, drafting and rewriting. After all, lucid prose can be just as dull, stale or clichéd as unclear prose. We will be looking at a much greater range of prose styles in this chapter, and particularly at writing that has lost its effectiveness because it is clichéd or overwritten. What techniques can be used to make language fresh and lively?

Cliché in speech and writing

One way of defining a cliché would be to call it 'prefabricated phrasing'; it is important to remember, though, that most clichés have usually been lively and arresting at some point and that's why they have passed into common usage. Clichéd writing is not always ineffective writing: it depends entirely on what is being done with it. Some contemporary post-modern writers and film-makers use cliché in inventive and surprising ways – in order to create parody or comedy or to draw attention to the fact that language and ideas are never original but are endlessly being recycled. The playwright and novelist Samuel Beckett wrote a play in 1961 called *Happy Days*, in which he presents us with a woman buried up to her waist in a mound of scorched grass. Very little happens in the play except that Winnie talks to herself about anything and everything and goes through the contents of her shopping bag; by the second act she is buried up to her neck in the mound. Winnie's talk is full of the 'prefabricated phrases' of everyday life, advertising and popular song – expressions such as 'no better no worse', 'can't be helped', 'mustn't complain'. Even the title phrase itself refers to the music-hall song 'Happy Days Are Here Again'. Through the tenacity and stoical cheerfulness of Winnie's words, Beckett seems to be testifying to the vitality and endurance of a common 'folk' language in the face of death.

ACTIVITY 1:

Write a monologue using a series of clichés to parody a fictional character of your choice. You might want to use a sportsman or woman being interviewed after a race, football or tennis match, or a politician canvassing for votes before an election, for instance.

We all use prefabricated phrases in everyday life. After all, it's not easy being original in every exchange we have with other people. 'How are you?' 'I'm fine thanks, and you?' is an exchange that we use many times a day as we make our way around our schools, colleges, universities or the local neighbourhood. There are variations in the register ('all right, mate?' 'yeah, I'm all right') but the exchange is almost identical. The exchange serves its function as a greeting, but does not mean very much in itself. The language is not being used in fresh and exciting ways – it doesn't need to be. The words are less important than the greeting and the exchange.

It is difficult sometimes not to be clichéd. For instance, when we want to console someone about a bereavement or the break-up of a relationship it is often a struggle to find something to say that sounds sincere. Over and over again we can find that the things we want to say come out as clichés because the situation we are trying to address is such a common one. Here are some examples of clichés people use to console themselves or others about a situation that has gone wrong. Some of them are more jaded than others.

> There's harmony in disharmony
> It could be worse
> Tomorrow is another day
> I will survive
> Every cloud has a silver lining
> There's a light at the end of the tunnel
> After the rain comes a rainbow
> It's always darkest before the dawn
> It has to get worse, before it gets better
> Every rose has its thorn
> It's not the end of the world
> Life's not so bad, when you consider the alternative
> The sharper the berry, the sweeter the wine

Sometimes people misuse clichés in speech in interesting ways. A United States senator, for example, trying to reassure his constituents that the budget talks were going well in spite of the apparent chaos, told reporters, 'It's always darkest before the storm', rather than 'before the dawn'. The original sentence 'It's always darkest before the dawn' means that the darkness heralds dawn – there is hope. The new sentence 'It's always darkest before the storm' suggests that this darkness is going to be followed by even worse events. As a verbal slip the misused cliché was probably more truthful than the intended meaning.

Here is another set of clichés that people use to console themselves about unrequited or lost love in both speech and writing:

> S/he'll be sorry
> S/he wasn't worth it anyway
> I'm better off alone
> There are plenty more fish in the sea
> Love hurts
> One lost, ten found
> It's better to have loved and lost than never to have loved at all
> All's fair in love and war

ACTIVITY 2:

Contemporary pop-songs are sometimes fresh and original and sometimes packed with cliché and usually somewhere in between. Writing with originality about love has always been very difficult because the feelings and situations have already been described thousands of times before in novels, songs and poetry – feelings about loving someone who doesn't love you, about seeing someone you love with someone else, about loving two people at the same time, about wishing someone would notice you. Here are some examples of song lyrics about love. Examine the lyrics looking particularly for originality of expression. Write a short report about the use of language in the two songs.

Love is All Around
By The Troggs

(Lyrics Courtesy of Kipp Teague's Lyric Archive, http://www.retroweb.com/lyrics)

I feel it in my fingers, I feel it in my toes
Love is all around me and so the feeling grows
It's written on the wind, it's everywhere I go
So if you really love me, come on and let it show

You know I love you I always will
My mind's made up by the way that I feel
There's no beginning, there'll be no end
'Cause on my love you can depend

I see your face before me, as I lay on my bed
I kinda get to thinking of all the things we said
You gave a promise to me, and I gave mine to you
I need someone beside me in everything I do

You know I love you I always will
My mind's made up by the way that I feel
There's no beginning, there'll be no end
'Cause on my love you can depend

It's written on the wind, it's everywhere I go
So if you really love me, come on and let it show
Come on and let it show

A Case of You
By Joni Mitchell

(http://www.jonimitchell.com/Blue71LyricsHome.html)

Just before our love got lost you said,
'I am as constant as a northern star.'
And I said, 'Constantly in the darkness
Where's that at?
If you want me I'll be in the bar.'
On the back of a cartoon coaster
In the blue TV screen light
I drew a map of Canada
Oh Canada
With your face sketched on it twice
Oh, you're in my blood like holy wine
You taste so bitter and so sweet
Oh I could drink a case of you, darling
And I would still be on my feet
Oh I would still be on my feet

Oh I am a lonely painter
I live in a box of paints
I'm frightened by the devil
And I'm drawn to those ones that ain't afraid
I remember that time you told me, you said,
'Love is touching souls'
Surely you touched mine
'Cause part of you pours out of me
In these lines from time to time
Oh, you're in my blood like holy wine
You taste so bitter and so sweet
Oh I could drink a case of you, darling
Still, I'd be on my feet
I would still be on my feet

©1971 BY JONI MITCHELL/BMI

ACTIVITY 3:

Now look at this love sonnet by William Shakespeare. In the sixteenth century many Elizabethan sonneteers imitated the Italian poet Petrarch in using a series of Petrarchan conceits (comparisons or elaborate parallels between two very dissimilar things or situations). Although in the hands of Petrarch these conceits had been striking and illuminating comparisons, they had become so overused in the sonnets of his imitators that they had become clichéd. Shakespeare parodies some of these conceits in the following sonnet. How does Shakespeare address the subject of cliché and originality in this poem?

Sonnet 130

My mistress' eyes are nothing like the sun;
Coral is far more red than her lips' red;
If snow be white, why then her breasts are dun;
If hairs be wires, black wires grow on her head.
I have seen roses damasked, red and white,
But no such roses see I in her cheeks;
And in some perfumes there is more delight
Than in the breath that from my mistress reeks.
I love to hear her speak, yet well I know
That music hath a far more pleasing sound;
I grant I never saw a goddess go;
My mistress, when she walks, treads on the ground.
And yet, by heav'n, I think my love as rare
As any she belied with false compare.

(Shakespeare 1977: 112)

ACTIVITY 4:

Below are two passages describing a kiss. Such scenes are notoriously difficult to write without being clichéd. Compare the two passages, paying particular attention to individual words, phrases and expressions. Analyse certain sections in both passages to argue that the writers use language in a fresh or inventive way or in a clichéd or predictable way – or perhaps in both ways. The first piece is from a popular romance by Carole Mortimer, written in 1984, and the second was written by D.H. Lawrence in 1921. Consider how far your responses depend upon previous reading and what is or is not familiar to particular readers at particular times.

She had no premonition as she opened the door, no warning of the shock she was to receive when she saw the identity of her visitor. Her mouth fell open in surprise, her face paling, the golden eyes suddenly huge in her drawn face.

At that moment she wished she could deny all knowledge of the man standing outside the door, but the lean body in the casual denims and short leather jacket, the ruggedly attractive face dominated by laughing blue eyes, the overlong dark hair with its auburn highlights were all too familiar. Jared Rourke!

'Hello, Kate,' he greeted softly, in a well-educated voice, although it did not indicate public school like Richard's did.

She wished she could have answered him, but for the moment she seemed to have lost her voice – something that had never happened to her before. What was he doing here? More to the point, what was she going to do with him when Richard was waiting for her in the lounge?

Jared felt no such inhibitions about his own actions, and stepped forward, taller than her by at least six inches at six foot two, his arms like steel vices as he took her in his arms, his mouth claiming hers with arrogant possession.

Kate felt herself respond to him as she had from their first meeting, having no strength to fight him as his mouth moved over hers with drugging insistence, laying intimate claim to her lips, while his hands moved over her body with sure deliberation.

'Mm,' he pulled back slightly, resting his forehead on hers as he looked down at her, a growth of copper-coloured beard on his chin evidence of his need for a shave. 'I needed that,' he spoke softly, his voice husky.

(Mortimer 1984: 8–9)

She seemed to faint beneath, and he seemed to faint, stooping over her. It was a perfect passing away for both of them, and at the same time the most intolerable accession into being, the marvellous fullness of immediate gratification, overwhelming, outflooding, from the source of the deepest life-force, the darkest, deepest, strangest life-force of the human body, at the back and the base of the loins.

After a lapse of stillness, after the rivers of strange dark fluid richness had passed over her, flooding, carrying away her mind and flooding down her spine and down her knees, past her feet, a strange flood, sweeping away everything and leaving her an essential new being, she was left quite free, she was free in complete ease, her complete self. So she rose, stilly and blithe, smiling at him. He stood before her, glimmering, so awfully real, that her heart almost stopped beating. He stood there in his strange, whole body, that had its marvellous fountains, like the bodies of the sons of God who were in the beginning.

(Lawrence 1973: 354)

All words have been used millions and millions of times before, but sometimes they cluster together into groups which become so overused we hardly hear their original meaning any more. However, a good deal of verbal art from children's rhymes to jokes to formulaic poetry and narrative depends upon repeated and well-loved phrases, plot lines or stories. Indeed, in a strict sense, any metrical form or any recurrent phrase or story motif is a cliché in that it is prefabricated. Such prefabricated ideas or phrases or stories can be constraining for a writer, but they can also offer opportunities for new ideas and associations. Many of the phrases that we use in the form of metaphors or figures of speech or aphorisms had original meanings but their significance is lost to us because we live in a different time and place: 'flogging a dead horse', 'barking up the wrong tree', 'killing two birds with one stone', 'a red herring', 'a stitch in time saves nine'. Brewer's *Dictionary of Phrase and Fable* (1995) will tell you the origin of such phrases. For instance, the saying 'don't look a gift horse in the mouth' refers to the custom of judging the age of a horse by its teeth. Hence the saying means 'if someone gives you something free don't be too picky about its value or quality'.

These are metaphors which have lost their original context, but somehow we all still understand what they mean and for a writer they can offer opportunities for puns, parody or poetry. They are called dead metaphors, but dead metaphors, as James Joyce once pointed out, can leave behind 'ghosts' of their original meanings.

Overwriting

Sometimes writing can be ineffective as a result not of the use of clichés but of overwriting. Critics and reviewers sometimes use the term 'purple prose' to describe writing that is, in their opinion, overburdened with adjectives and adverbs so that it is too rich, too full of ingredients like a piece of fruit cake. Such writing can also be clichéd and laboured, but sometimes it can be both overblown and inventive at the same time. So much again depends upon purpose and context. Baroque or ornate prose styles can be very effective in fiction such as the writing of Angela Carter. The following passage is from the opening paragraph of Carter's short story 'The Erl-King' from her collection of gothic fairy stories *The Bloody Chamber*:

> The lucidity, the clarity of the light that afternoon was sufficient to itself; perfect transparency might be impenetrable, these vertical bars of a brass-coloured distillation of light coming down from sulphur-yellow interstices in a sky hunkered with grey clouds that bulge with more rain. It struck the wood with nicotine-stained fingers, the leaves glittered. A cold day of late October, when the withered blackberries dangled like their own dour spooks on the discoloured brambles. There were crisp husks of beechmast and cast acorn cups underfoot in the russet slime of dead bracken where the rains of the equinox had so soaked the earth that the cold oozed up through the soles of the shoes, lancinating cold of the approach of winter that grips hold of your belly and squeezes it tight. Now the stark elders have an anorexic look; there is not much in the autumn wood to make you smile but it is not yet, not quite yet, the saddest time of the year. Only, there is a haunting sense of the imminent cessation of being; the year, in turning, turns in on itself. Introspective weather, a sickroom hush.
>
> (Carter 1981: 84)

In the United States there is an annual competition called the Bulwer-Lytton contest for turgid fiction, named after the Victorian novelist who began one of his novels with the immortal words 'It was a dark and stormy night'. This is perhaps a rather unfair title for the competition as although Bulwer-Lytton did write extravagant prose, nonetheless even the opening words 'It was a dark and stormy night' were arresting and successful when they were first used. Here is one of the winning entries from the Bulwer-Lytton contest, noted perhaps less for its clichés than for being an example of 'overblown' prose. However, you might argue that the extended simile for the shattered computer terminal is very striking: 'like a silicon armadillo left to rot on the information superhighway'.

> As the fading light of a dying day filtered through the window blinds, Roger stood over his victim with a smoking .45, surprised at the serenity that filled him after pumping six slugs into the bloodless tyrant that had mocked him day after day, and then he shuffled out of the office with one last look back at the shattered computer terminal lying there like a silicon armadillo left to rot on the information superhighway.
>
> (Larry Brill – www.bulwer-lytton.com)

Even academic writers, often noted for their use of analytical and spare prose styles, can produce extravagant prose. The following sentence from a published academic essay by Stephen T. Tyman, called 'Ricoeur and the Problem of Evil', is just such an example:

> With the last gasp of Romanticism, the quelling of its florid uprising against the vapid formalism of one strain of the Enlightenment, the dimming of its yearning for the imagined grandeur of the archaic, and the dashing of its too sanguine hopes for a revitalized, fulfilled humanity, the horror of its more lasting, more Gothic legacy has settled in, distributed and diffused enough, to be sure, that lugubriousness is recognizable only as languor, or as a certain sardonic laconicism disguising itself in a new sanctification of the destructive instincts, a new genius for displacing cultural reifications in the interminable shell game of the analysis of the human psyche, where nothing remains sacred.
>
> (Tyman 1995: 74)

Here is another entry submitted to the Bulwer-Lytton contest (it is an example of journalism by the *San Jose Mercury News* writer Patrick May):

> Shrouded in Winter fog, trapped in the gullies of the Mother Lode, the ghosts of a thousand mining camps toss in a fitful slumber. Down in Dead Mule Cañon, up on Chicken-Thief Flat, the pick and shovel clang in muffled knell. A century and a half after that first golden glint caught James Marshall's eye, after the lust and liquor scattered lost souls over every hill and hollow, these foothills still tremble . . . The Gold Rush was the largest mass migration in American history. It was the champagne bottle smashed over California's bow.
>
> (*San Jose Mercury News*, 18 January 1998 – www.bulwer-lytton.com)

The author of the following extract from a romantic thriller is a certain Joan Collins. It was also submitted to the contest. After paying a large amount of money to commission the novel, the publishers finally rejected it:

> 'And this,' Pauline continued, indicating the largest of the three men, 'is Mr. Earl. He's your security guard, and he'll shadow you until the jewels are returned all in one piece.'
> Laura smiled charmingly at the beefy young guard, whose massive shoulders and biceps threatened to split the seams of his rented dinner jacket.
> ''Ello, Miss,' he said, politely touching his forehead with a finger in a kind of salute. 'It's a right 'onor. 'Course, my old mum an' I, we seen all yer pictures. She's a great fan 'o yers, is me mum.'
>
> (Joan Collins, *Hell Hath No Fury* (unpublished) – www.bulwer-lytton.com)

ACTIVITY 5:

Of course, just because a piece of prose has been submitted for a competition such as the Bulwer-Lytton does not necessarily mean that the passage is ineffective on its own terms or for the audience for whom it was written. Choose one of the passages above which you think has been unfairly maligned and argue that it is effective.

ACTIVITY 6:

Why might writing a review of a piece of music or a bottle of wine be particularly challenging? How might such reviewers find ways of describing what they hear or taste? Find a review of a piece of music in a music magazine or a wine in a wine magazine. Identify words, phrases or parts of sentences that you find particularly effective and discuss why these work. Pay particular attention to the effects achieved by combining particular words. Also consider why parts of your chosen passage might be considered 'purple prose', if appropriate.

Refreshing words: drafting

We said in the introduction that this book, like all books, has passed through many stages in the production process. It began as teaching notes many years ago and has evolved into course materials which we gave to students and finally into what you see here: a published book in a series of four. Some sections of the book have survived from the very earliest stages of the writing section and some sections were added at a very late stage, but all sections have been redrafted at least twice. Most of this redrafting has been done on a word-processor, but at each crucial stage we have printed out a copy and added hand-written editing notes, corrections, alterations and additions to the print-out, and often asked other readers to add their comments and adjustments. Then we returned to the word-processor to make the changes to the original text. There are many ways of drafting work depending upon a number of factors, including the purpose and context of the writing and the size of the document. These days few writers work solely with hand-written materials – most will be using word-processors in some way.

Redrafting is the process of producing a new draft from a previous draft – re-reading it and thinking about how you want to change it. Sometimes it involves receiving comments from others and then deciding whether you accept these suggestions or not. Re-reading your own work helps you to see your ideas and the way you have expressed them at more of a distance and to see where the weaknesses lie. Redrafting can give you an opportunity to let others see your work and to comment on it, and these people might see things that you have missed – areas where the writing has lost its clarity, or where the expression is weak or where the writing has become pretentious or muddled. Because this book addresses general writing skills and not the specific skills needed for, say, essay writing or short story writing, we will only point out some general principles for effective editing and drafting here.

- Reviewing work on paper is usually more effective as for some reason it is easier to spot mistakes on the page and it also gives you an opportunity to mark these mistakes and make notes for additions, corrections or alterations in the writing.
- You will probably find that you can edit your own work more easily if you have printed out the writing in double rather than single spacing.
- If you are redrafting a long piece of work, it's probably a good idea to do so in sections so that you bring a fresh eye to the whole document.
- Read your draft aloud to yourself – this will help you establish a sense of audience and a voice. Underline any phrases or expressions that sound awkward or unclear in some way and add a note to yourself to change the phrasing or the structure of the sentence. A good check is to look for where you stumble in reading the piece aloud. If you stumble or if you have to go back and read a sentence or paragraph again to make sense of it, you will probably need to redraft that section, but after you have worked out what's wrong with it first. The sentence may be too long or the syntax might need rearranging or there may be something missing (such as a verb or a link to the previous sentence or paragraph).

As you review your writing (of whatever kind – creative, academic, journalistic, for instance) ask yourself some of the following questions:

- What is the function of the piece of writing? What is your aim?
- Who is it written for – what is the assumed audience?
- Is the language you have chosen (tone, pitch, register, choice of vocabulary, sentence structure) appropriate for the purpose and the audience?
- Have you achieved your aims? If not, why not? What still needs to be done?
- Is the structure appropriate for the aims of the piece of writing? Would a restructuring of certain sections help to make it work better?
- Do the divisions into paragraphs work? Do the paragraph breaks come at the right places – when the discussion or subject matter changes direction?
- Is the prose style appropriate for the purpose, context and audience? If not, why not, and what do you need to do to change it?

You will need to read the writing through at least once, checking for all these different aspects – prose style, structure, paragraph breaks. If you can find someone else to read it through at the same time, make sure you tell him or her what you would like them to look for. You might tell them, for instance, that you are not entirely happy with the prose style of the piece or you might ask them to mark the parts of the writing which they think are overwritten. Alternatively you might ask them to check for clarity or structural coherence.

Over the next few pages we have assembled some of the suggestions for drafting skills given to writers in a number of advice manuals published this century. Some of these repeat the principles of the Plain English Campaign, but we have tried to highlight here some principles for avoiding clichéd or overblown prose and for controlling the rhythms and sounds of what you write as well as the content. It should be seen as a continuation of the principles and guidelines for effective writing outlined in the last chapter.

Vary sentence patterns

Avoid monotony by varying sentence patterns. If you always use sentences with the same or similar structure, the result may sound tedious. One of the best ways to avoid a dull series of simple sentences is to use subordination to combine the information presented in these sentences into a single, complex sentence. For example:

> The Challenge project is run by Parkside School. It was set up in 1985. One of its aims is to give the students at the school an opportunity to serve the local community. Another aim is to develop their confidence and key skills.

becomes

> The Challenge project, established in 1985 by Parkside School, aims to give its students the opportunity to serve their community and to develop their confidence and key skills.

However, compound and complex sentences can themselves become tedious, and sometimes they are awkward or confusing. Don't overload your sentences or your readers. If you find a sentence is becoming too long and confusing, or if you have used three or four complex sentences in a row, reverse the process described above and break your sentence up into several shorter sentences.

Variation in other sentence features such as openings and sentence length is equally important. Read your piece of writing aloud to yourself and listen out for rhythm in particular. A good combination of types of sentence will usually ensure a good rhythm and pace.

Choose your words carefully

The English language includes over one million words. It is the largest lexicon in the world and from it English-speakers choose the precise words to meet their needs. Choosing the right type of word for the right occasion with so many choices available, however, is not always easy. Conrad described his struggle with language this way in his Preface to the novel *The Nigger of the 'Narcissus'* (1897):

> it is only through an unremitting never-discouraged care for the shape and ring of sentences that an approach can be made to plasticity, to colour, and the light of a magic suggestiveness can be brought to play for an evanescent instant over the commonplace surface of words: of the old, old words, worn thin, defaced by ages of careless usage.
>
> (Conrad 1977: iv)

So the daily business of the writer is often the search for the right word, the right place in the sentence, the right combination of words to create a language that is vital rather than jaded. This involves drafting and redrafting. You might want to consider the following points.

The Plain English Campaign rightly insists that the effectiveness of some writing depends upon simplicity and directness. If your primary aim is accessibility, heed the advice of William Strunk and E.B. White in their famous manual, *The Elements of Style,* first published in 1918:

If those who have studied the art of writing are in accord on any one point, it is on this: the surest way to arouse and hold the attention of the reader is by being *specific, definite, and concrete*. The greatest writers . . . are effective largely because they deal in particulars and report the details that matter. Their words call up pictures. [our italics]

(Strunk and White 1979: 74)

So, when your aim is clarity, avoid the kind of inflated prose found in this memo:

Pursuant to the recent memorandum issued August 9, 1979, because of petroleum exigencies, it is incumbent upon us all to endeavour to make maximal utilisation of telephonic communication in lieu of personal visitation.

and instead be more direct:

As the memo of August 9 said: during the petrol shortage try to use the telephone as much as you can instead of making personal visits.

Choose the word most appropriate for the task in hand. If you are writing descriptive prose you will be working a good deal with adjectives. However, if you are writing informative prose your need for adjectives will be considerably lessened. Imagine a set of instructions for a flat-pack set of shelves flooded with adjectives. They would not only be out-of-place but would be a positive hindrance.

Think about sound and rhythm when choosing words. All other things being equal, you may want to choose one word rather than another simply because you like its sound or rhythm. Although what you are writing may never be read aloud, most readers do 'hear' what they read via an inner voice. Hence, the 'sound' of your writing can add to or detract from its flow and thus influence the reader's impression of what you have written. Rhythm can contribute to the flow of your writing, and a sudden break in rhythm can create emphasis. Finally, note that rhythm is especially important in parallel structures and is often a factor in sentence-to-sentence flow; that is, you must read a sequence of sentences in context to judge their rhythm. We will look at rhythm in prose writing in more detail in the next chapter.

Finally, try to extend your vocabulary. Use a thesaurus and a dictionary to help with this. In your reading note the words you don't know, look them up and memorise them so you can try them in your writing.

ACTIVITY 7:

Re-read the passage from Angela Carter's short story 'The Erl-King'. Identify all the words she uses which are either unusual in themselves or which are unusual in combination with other words. Look up any words you don't know. How effective is this passage, in your opinion, in describing the winter landscape of her fairy story? What images and word combinations do you find most effective? Write a short analysis of the passage. Then rewrite it in order to experiment with alternative words and word combinations. Use a thesaurus to find alternative words.

The lucidity, the clarity of the light that afternoon was sufficient to itself; perfect transparency might be impenetrable, these vertical bars of a brass-coloured distillation of light coming down from sulphur-yellow interstices in a sky hunkered with grey clouds that bulge with more rain. It struck the wood with nicotine-stained fingers, the leaves glittered. A cold day of late October, when the withered blackberries dangled like their own dour spooks on the discoloured brambles. There were crisp husks of beechmast and cast acorn cups underfoot in the russet slime of dead bracken where the rains of the equinox had so soaked the earth that the cold oozed up through the soles of the shoes, lancinating cold of the approach of winter that grips hold of your belly and squeezes it tight. Now the stark elders have an anorexic look; there is not much in the autumn wood to make you smile but it is not yet, not quite yet, the saddest time of the year. Only, there is a haunting sense of the imminent cessation of being; the year, in turning, turns in on itself. Introspective weather, a sickroom hush.

(Carter 1979: 84)

As we have said, writing decisions depend upon context and purpose. Most writers will spend much of their time searching for new clusters of words that will express something more sharply and precisely. Joseph Conrad is an interesting case here because he chose to write in English and not Polish, his first language, or French, his second. A friend of his, the writer Ford Madox Ford, claimed that Conrad chose to write in English because he believed that:

no English word is a word ... all English words are instruments for exciting blurred emotions. 'Oaken' in French means 'made of oak wood' – nothing more. 'Oaken' in English connotes numerous moral attributes ... The consequence is, that no English word has clean edges: a reader is always, for a fraction of a second, uncertain as to which meaning of the word the writer may intend. Thus all English prose is blurred.

(Ford 1924: 214)

In other words suggestiveness is something that Conrad, like other writers, worked towards not through precision but by a deliberate blurring of meaning. The fact that a certain word has many associations and echoes is often very useful for a writer of poetry or fiction, but it might inhibit the writing of analytical prose.

Avoid overusing modifiers

Make sure that your use of modifiers (adjectives or adverbs that 'modify' the noun or verb in the sentence) is appropriate for the purpose and context of your writing. You will need to avoid overusing adjectives and adverbs in most writing, particularly writing that needs to be economical with words. Modifiers have their place (in descriptive writing, for instance), but in the most vigorous prose, action is expressed in verbs, and the agents of that action are expressed in nouns. This principle applies to both ornate modifiers and such commonplace intensifiers as 'really', 'pretty' and 'very'.

Prune deadwood

Deadwood is material that adds nothing to the meaning of the sentence, words that serve only as filler. When you edit your writing, eliminate any words or phrases that can be removed without damaging the meaning of the sentence or paragraph:

> I spent my first six weeks at university in a state of shock, but today I have a completely different perspective on the institution in general, as compared to when I first started.

becomes:

> I spent my first six weeks 'at university in a state of shock, but today I have a completely different perspective on the institution.

Use metaphor to illustrate but avoid cliché

Metaphor may be broadly defined as an imaginative comparison, expressed or implied, between two generally unlike things, for the purpose of illustration.

By this definition, similes (a comparison of one object to another) are a subset of metaphor. In prose (as opposed to poetry), metaphors are most often used to illustrate, and thus make clear, abstract ideas:

> When two atoms approach each other at great speeds they go through one another, while at moderate speeds they bound off each other like two billiard balls.

Whenever you use figurative language, be careful to avoid clichés. If you can't think of a fresh, imaginative way to express an idea, it's better to express it in literal terms than to resort to cliché. Hence, 'Solving the problem was as easy as pie' becomes 'Solving the problem was easy'.

Proof-read

> A scrupulous writer, in every sentence that he writes, will ask himself at least four questions, thus: What am I trying to say? What words will express it? What image or idiom will make it clearer? Is this image fresh enough to have an effect? And he will probably ask himself two more: Could I put it more shortly? Have I said anything that is avoidably ugly?
>
> (Orwell 1950: 95)

No matter how many times you read through a 'finished' piece of writing, you are likely to miss many of your most frequent errors, so take time over proof-reading and consider the following:

- Allow yourself some time between writing and proofing. Even a five-minute break is productive because it will help get some distance from what you have written. The goal is to return with a fresh eye and mind.
- Reading aloud will help you hear mistakes as well as see them.
- Be aware of the mistakes you usually make and search for those in particular.
- Remember to check for coherence and cohesion as well as the 'little' errors such as apostrophes.
- When you read through the final draft of your essay, take a pen and mark it as if you were your tutor. This will help you to have a critical eye and to be a rigorous editor of your own work.
- Put a line under every single word, phrase or sentence that seems clumsy or which jars on your ear as you read. Then rewrite all those sections.

ACTIVITY 8:

Choose one of the extracts we have used in this chapter or a piece of your own recent writing (of whatever kind – academic writing, letter, journal, short story, poem) and redraft it at least three times. Consider the redrafting questions and advice on rewriting we have laid out in this chapter and analyse the first draft before you begin, defining exactly what you will try to achieve in rewriting it. At each stage provide a commentary on what you have added or changed in the draft and why you have chosen to do this. Use a thesaurus if you find it useful.

ACTIVITY 9:

The following is an extract from a university prospectus for an English literature degree programme. Identify the sentences that you think are the most effective and well-written. Are there any changes in the wording that you would want to make so that the piece sounds more inviting to prospective students? Produce several drafts, adding a commentary to each explaining what you were trying to do at each stage.

Cambridge City has a good ambience in which to study literature. A historic university town, it has the bookshops, theatres, specialist cinemas, art galleries, publishers, museums and concerts that that implies. It is crowded with literary associations; if the inn where Byron kept his pet bear has disappeared, Rupert Brooke's chestnut trees have not. You can still retrace the steps of Marlowe, Milton, Wordsworth, Tennyson, E.M. Forster, Virginia Woolf and Sylvia Plath.

Anglia is a very strong centre for English literature. The departmental staff offer expertise on an extremely wide range of periods and subjects. We are proud of our teaching experience and publications record. In January 1995 we had additional reason for pride when the Higher Education Funding Council awarded this course the rating of excellent.

(Anglia Polytechnic University Prospectus 1999/2000: 1)

Summary

In this chapter we have:

- reinforced the importance of knowing context, purpose and audience when writing
- studied clichés and how to avoid or use them in your own writing
- looked at examples of 'purple prose' and literary parodies
- considered ways of redrafting a text and stressed the importance of proof-reading.

References

Brewer, Ebenezer Cobham (1995) *Brewer's Dictionary of Phrase and Fable* [1870], 15th edn. London: HarperCollins.

Carter, Angela (1981) *The Bloody Chamber* [1979]. Harmondsworth: Penguin.

Conrad, Joseph (1977) *'The Nigger of the "Narcissus"'*, *'Typhoon' and Other Stories* [1897]. Harmondsworth: Penguin.

Ford, Ford Madox (1924) *Joseph Conrad: A Personal Remembrance*. London: Duckworth.

James, Henry (1957) 'The Art of Fiction' [1884] in *The House of Fiction: Essays on the Novel*, edited with an introduction by Leon Edel. London: Hart-Davis.

Lawrence, D.H. (1973) *Women in Love* [1921]. Harmondsworth: Penguin.

Mortimer, Carole (1984) *Sensual Encounter*. London: Mills and Boon.

Orwell, George (1950) 'Politics and the English Language' [1946] in *Shooting an Elephant and Other Essays*. London: Secker & Warburg.

Shakespeare, William (1977) *Shakespeare's Sonnets* [1564–1616]. London: Yale University Press.

Strunk, W. and White, E.B. (1979) *The Elements of Style* [1918]. New York: Macmillan; London: Collier Macmillan.

Tyman, S.T. (1995) 'Ricoeur and the Problem of Evil' in Lewis Edwin Hahn (ed.), *The Philosophy of Paul Ricoeur*. Chicago: Open Court.

The rhythms of prose

Simon Featherstone

R hythm, the sound of words and sentences, is a quality of writing normally associated with poetry. We are used to analysing the metre of verse and discussing its contribution to the total effect of the poem. When reading prose, though, it is the meaning rather than the sound that we tend to concentrate upon. This is probably because there is no break of line to alert us to the units of rhythm, we are less likely to hear the piece read out loud, and the subject matter of prose tends to emphasise narrative and information over sound and effect.

Nevertheless, despite all this, rhythm is as intrinsic to the effect of prose as it is to poetry. Whether we are reading fiction, letters, reports or essays, we are more likely to feel satisfied with the writing and understand fully what it says if the language has an underlying pulse. 'Reason persuades, but rhythm convinces', the poet C.H. Sisson once said, and to understand the truth of that we have to be able to listen to the often subtle rhythms of prose, see how other elements of language – word choice, syntax, punctuation – shape that rhythm, and understand what makes them effective in our own writing.

Listening for the voice

Here is a passage of fiction. It is the first paragraph of J.M. Coetzee's novel *In the Heart of the Country* (1977), which is written in the voice of a young woman living a lonely life on a farm in South Africa at the turn of the century. Read it aloud to yourself slowly once or twice and make a note of sounds or phrases or combinations of words which you find particularly rhythmically effective.

Today my father brought home his new bride. They came clip-clop across the flats in a dog-cart drawn by a horse with an ostrich-plume waving on its forehead, dusty after the long haul. Or perhaps they were drawn by two plumed donkeys, that is also possible. My father wore his black swallowtail coat and stovepipe hat, his bride a wide-brimmed sunhat and a white dress tight at waist and throat. More detail I cannot give unless I begin to embroider, for I was not watching. I was in my room, in the emerald semi-dark of the shuttered late afternoon, reading a book or, more likely, supine with a damp towel over my eyes fighting a migraine. I am the one who stays in her room reading or writing or fighting migraines. The colonies are full of girls like that, but none, I think, so extreme as I. My father is the one who paces the floorboards back and forth, back and forth in his slow black boots. And then, for a third, there is the new wife, who lies late abed. Those are the antagonists.

(Coetzee 1982: 1)

The first paragraph of any story introduces the reader to the world of the novel, and here we get a clear sense of the restricted life of the narrator and the angry precision of her observation of that life. Coetzee uses little or no imagery. Nor does he use unusual language; instead he relies on small details such as the ostrich plumes, and selected actions like the father pacing and the girl lying with the towel on her eyes to create the atmosphere. We are alerted to the feelings of oppressive isolation and simmering anger by similarly sparse means – the spareness of the description of the arrival, the admission of or even desire for 'extremity', the definition of the new family as consisting of 'antagonists'.

Underlying all these elements, though, is a careful deployment of rhythm. The first sentence is almost in verse metre, with four regular stresses, 'Todáy my fáther brought hóme his new bríde', a rhythmic pattern repeated at various points in the paragraph ('Í am the óne who stáys in her róom', for example). Such emphasis is part of a larger rhythmic shape of the passage, in which these lines are set within longer sentences, typically extended by a noun, adjective or verb phrase – 'dusty after the long haul', 'that is also possible', 'tight at waist and throat'. Such phrases add variety to the sound of the paragraph and suggest to us that the speaker relishes the poetry of the description that she is providing.

The last four sentences of the paragraph evoke the strange emotional state of the narrator, and once again the sound of the sentences contributes to their effect. The first of these begins quite colloquially, but ends with the 'poetic' four-stress pattern noted earlier: 'but nóne I thínk as extréme as Í'. The shift *rhythmically* performs the narrator's tendency throughout the novel to transform the ordinary into the melodramatic and wildly imaginative. The next sentence modulates to the less emphatic description of her father (though note the poetic device of the repetition of 'back and forth'), before returning to the four-stress pattern in 'And thén for a thírd, there ís the new wífe'. The paragraph ends tersely, with an off-hand comment that sets up the family as theatrical enemies: 'Those are the antagonists'. Coetzee, then, gives us a good deal of information about the emotional state of his narrator – her dreaminess, obsessive observation, menacing jealousy – but it is done as much through the varying rhythms of her statements as by direct pronouncement.

A more extravagant example of a similar strategy is the famous first line of Edgar Allen Poe's short story 'The Tell-Tale Heart' (*c*.1843). This story is told in the voice of a murderer who is eventually driven to confess his crime by his psychotic fantasy of his victim's heart beating ever more loudly in the house in which the body is concealed. Poe begins the story: 'True! – nervous – very, very dreadfully nervous I had been and am; but why *will* you say that I am mad?' (Poe 1978: 289). This statement is ostensibly intended to assure us of the narrator's sanity, but it actually convinces us of his madness. The latter effect is achieved by the rhythm and syntax of the sentence. Poe could have made his murderer say, 'Although people say I am mad, I am really only very nervous'. The logical organisation and fluent rhythm of this sentence might persuade us to keep an open mind about the speaker's true condition. As it stands, though, the initial exclamation, the exaggerated qualification of 'nervous', the odd placement of the main verbs 'had been' and 'am', and the emphasis on 'mad' at the end of the sentence, disrupt the orderly progress and rhythm of a conventional sentence. We are then janglingly alert for the bizarre confession that follows.

The rhythmic effects that we have described in the two examples are not, perhaps, immediately noticeable on a first reading. They exist beneath the surface of the prose like a pulse. We concentrate on making sense of an uneasy description, but what guides us through – and actually makes us more uneasy – are the shifting rhythms of the piece which reflect the disturbed minds of the narrators. In Coetzee's novel and Poe's story we are clearly dealing with voices that are not the authors' own, and so they are concerned to give us a definite sense of the features of that voice. But any piece of writing, whether it is a novel, a letter or an essay, *has a voice*, even if we are not actually reading the passage out loud. If the sound inside your head is an interesting one, you tend to listen to it. Good writers like Coetzee and Poe think about that internal sound, and can adjust the voice to suit particular purposes. Sometimes it is a kind of background hum, the engine ticking and running; sometimes the sound is more striking and noticeable; sometimes the sound reminds us of a particular place and time (some of the rhythms of *In the Heart of the Country*, for example, allude to nineteenth-century prose patterns, though they are never straightforward imitations). But whether immediately noticeable or not, it is a crucial part of the writing's effect, and the more we know about the rhythms that we and others are using, the more flexibility and force we can have in our reading and writing.

Choose a paragraph from a novel or short story which you think has a distinctive or interesting sound. Read it aloud and outline and define any distinctive rhythmic features that you notice as you read. Look for sentence length, syntax, pauses, accents, tone and emphasis. Alter the syntax and word order of a sentence in the passage. What effect does this have upon the voice and meaning of the passage? Write up your notes as a short commentary.

Rhythms in writing for the stage

Writing and speech are not as far apart as we might sometimes think. Even when we are reading silently, we hear a voice in our head performing the language on the page. Perhaps the best way to begin to think about the relationship between the two is to read plays. A play script is writing, but it only works when it is 'translated' into the sounds and rhythms of speech. To read a script we have to interpret the sounds created by the writer, supplying the particular intonations and stresses that best express our sense of the character. Much of this is done by our instinctive sense of the language, particularly if we are native speakers of that language. But in good drama there are always decisions to be made, sometimes between several possible ways of performing a speech. Each one might be valid, but each will give a different sense of the character and his or her story. To make these decisions we have to think carefully about the sound of prose.

The following passage is an extract from *The Homecoming* (1964) by Harold Pinter. Pinter's plays are difficult to perform, partly because there is very little information given about how a passage might be delivered, and partly because the dialogue is itself often puzzling and unexpected. This is the first meeting between Lenny and his sister-in-law Ruth, recently arrived from America. The only information Pinter gives us is that the meeting takes place in a house in North London and that the two characters are in their early thirties. The extract here follows on immediately from a long speech that Lenny makes to Ruth about his relationship with his brother and a strange, comically violent story that Lenny tells seemingly to shock her. There are perhaps indications of a London accent in his narrative, and the fact that he states admiration for his brother's education suggests that he himself didn't receive one. However, we also hear a man who can use language skilfully to dominate and bully. As the scene progresses, however, Ruth reveals her own linguistic powers.

Lenny: . . . Excuse me, shall I take this ashtray out of your way?

Ruth: It's not in my way.

Lenny: It seems to be in the way of your glass. The glass was about to fall. Or the ashtray. I'm rather worried about the carpet. It's not me, it's my father. He's obsessed with order and clarity. He doesn't like mess. So, as I don't believe you're smoking at the moment, I'm sure you won't object if I move the ashtray.

He does so.

And now perhaps I'll relieve you of your glass.

Ruth: I haven't quite finished.

Lenny: You've consumed quite enough, in my opinion.

Ruth: No, I haven't.

Lenny: Quite sufficient, in my own opinion.

Ruth: Not in mine, Leonard.

Pause.

Lenny: Don't call me that, please.

Ruth: Why not?

Lenny: That's the name my mother gave me.

Pause.

Just give me the glass.

Ruth: No.

Pause.

Lenny: I'll take it, then.

Ruth: If you take the glass . . . I'll take you.

Pause.

Lenny: How about me taking the glass without you taking me?

Ruth: Why don't I just take you?

Pause.

Lenny: You're joking.

Pause.

You're in love, anyway, with another man. You've had a secret liaison with another man. His family didn't even know. Then you come here without a word of warning and start to make trouble.

She picks up the glass and lifts it towards him.

Ruth: Have a sip. Go on. Have a sip from my glass.

He is still.

Sit on my lap. Take a long cool sip.

She pats her lap. Pause.

She stands, moves to him with the glass.

Put your head back and open your mouth.

Lenny: Take that glass away from me.

Ruth: Lie on the floor. Go on. I'll pour it down your throat.

Lenny: What are you doing, making me some kind of proposal?

She laughs shortly, drains the glass.

Ruth: Oh, I was thirsty.

She smiles at him, puts the glass down, goes into the hall and up the stairs. He
follows into the hall and shouts up the stairs.
Lenny: What was that supposed to be? Some kind of proposal?
Silence.
He comes back into the room, goes to his own glass, drains it.

(Pinter 1978: 49–51)

It is clear that a strange struggle for power is taking place, a struggle that touches upon dangerous issues of family history, sexual control and gender roles. Language is used in a kind of game to assert and repel, and we are given little overt guidance as to how this contest is to be performed. As readers or performers we need to decide on the kinds of voices the characters have – their accents and mannerisms, the tones of voice, and the volume, pace and emphasis of each of their contributions – and to do so we have to enter into the rhythms of those voices.

ACTIVITY 2:

As the scene progresses, the rhythmic decisions that the actors have to make multiply. What is the pacing of the dialogue? What pauses are required in it? How are its extreme shifts in register and tone to be managed in performance and to what effect? How do Ruth's increasingly effective responses and questions contrast in performance to Lenny's verbal strategy? Very small inflections and silences can alter the rhythm and hence the meaning of the scene.

Imagine you are directing a performance of Pinter's *The Homecoming*. Make detailed notes to prepare actors for performance. You will need to decide upon such things as emphasis, pauses, speed, intonation and tone. For each decision that you take, make clear the effect that you are trying to achieve and how it will contribute to the drama. Mark out some of the sentences with stress marks and indications of the length of pauses to show how you want them to be delivered. (If you are working in groups, perform your version of the script in pairs, revising and adjusting the rhythm until you achieve the effects that you want. Watch others in your group perform the same scene, and discuss the different decisions that you took and the different effects that you were able to achieve). Write up your notes as a set of performance notes from the director to a group of actors who are meeting to begin rehearsing this short scene.

Rhythm for rhythm's sake

In Pinter, Poe and Coetzee's work we have seen prose rhythm underpinning the effect and meaning of narrative and performance. Other writers use rhythm more overtly and for different reasons. This is a piece of prose by the American writer Gertrude Stein entitled 'A Portrait of One: Harry Phelan Gibb' (1922):

> Some one in knowing everything is knowing that some one is something. Some one is something and is succeeding is succeeding in hoping that thing. He is suffering.
>
> He is succeeding in hoping and he is succeeding in saying that that is something. He is suffering, he is suffering and succeeding in hoping that in succeeding in saying that he is succeeding in hoping is something.
>
> He is suffering, he is hoping, he is succeeding in saying that anything is something. He is suffering, he is hoping, he is succeeding in saying that anything is something. He is suffering, he is hoping, he is succeeding in saying that something is something. He is hoping that he is succeeding in hoping that something is something. He is hoping that he is succeeding in saying that he is succeeding in hoping that something is something. He is hoping that he is succeeding in saying that something is something.

> (Stein 1968: 201)

At first glance, the passage looks like conventional prose and, though the title is a little obscure, we might nevertheless think that we are to get an impression, a portrait in words, of a person or character called Harry Phelan Gibb. We soon realise, though, that we are not to receive any 'prosaic' information. What we get instead are sentences that recycle a limited number of words and grammatical patterns. These just about make sense in isolation, but it is impossible to paraphrase the passage as a whole or to relate them to the stated topic of the title. As a result, the more we read the less we notice what is being said and the more we notice the sound and intonation of the sentences. This is, of course, very unusual. As we have seen, prose rhythm is normally implied, a background music to meaning that we detect only when we listen for it. Here there is no meaning, and Stein forces us to listen to phrasing and stress patterns of language, making rhythm the focus of reading rather than a hidden component.

You might try to define your response to reading such material. Frequent reactions are bemusement, irritation and amusement, as adult readers are made to take part in apparently nonsensical word games. Stein, quite deliberately, stripped her prose of its seriousness and intellectual meanings, and restored the pleasures of sound and play, making her readers relearn the sounds and pulses of a language. In her work, the rhythms that normally lie beneath sense are dominant, and her readers are returned to the condition of children encountering the strangeness and pleasure of language in itself, rather than experiencing language as merely a vehicle for communication.

ACTIVITY 3:

Choose a sentence or phrase that you have often heard a friend, relative or acquaintance say, and that sticks in your memory, or a line or two of a song, rhyme or jingle. Using Gertrude Stein's 'game' as a model, construct a short piece of writing which explores the variations of sound and rhythm in that piece of language. Remember this is an exercise in sound, rather than sense, so don't be afraid to push the syntax as far beyond the everyday as you care to. What rhythmic possibilities are there in everyday language? Write a commentary explaining what you were trying to do.

Rhythm and comedy

The explorations of rhythmic play and rhythmic control that we saw in Stein's and Pinter's work often come together in the language use of comedians and comic writers. The variety comedian Jimmy James once said that a comedian is someone who says things funnily, not someone who says funny things, suggesting that the skill of the comic is not just in thinking of funny ideas, but in their shaping and delivery. Jokes and funny stories that are hilarious when told by one person can be dull and embarrassing when told by somebody else. What makes the difference is the tellers' control of pace, emphasis and intonation. Good comedians are always masters of rhythm – or timing as it's often called. This is not just a matter of knowing when to pause or when to move to a punch-line; it is also a question of selecting words that *sound* funny, and organising the syntax of a sentence so that these words are rhythmically effective.

To illustrate how fundamental rhythm is to humour we can examine a Woody Allen one-liner: 'Sex without love is an empty experience, but as empty experiences go, it's one of the best'. The sentence is funny partly because of what it says – the apparently moralising beginning is undercut by the final chirpy acceptance of the pleasures of the 'empty experience'. But it is also funny because of its rhythm and organisation. Imagine if Woody Allen had said 'Sex without love is an empty experience, but it's one of the best as empty experiences go'. This sentence communicates the same idea as the first, but it is not as funny. The joke needs 'as empty experiences go' as an embedded clause to delay the punchline, to give a pleasing symmetry to the sentence, and to ensure that the emphasis falls upon the surprise word, 'best'. Of course, Woody Allen probably did not analyse his rhythm and syntax as I have done. Like all the best comedians, he has an instinct for the most effective way of shaping a sentence to achieve the effect that he wants – laughter.

The English comedian Victoria Wood comes from a different comic tradition from that of Woody Allen, but she, too, works through careful rhythmic patternings of language to create humour. Wood's character comedy is based upon the speech-patterns of her native Lancashire; the following extract from a dialogue between her teenage character Kelly-Marie Tunstall and her pal at a bus-stop illustrates how Wood slightly exaggerates the inflections of everyday language for comic effect:

Kelly: So he walked over, right, big 'I am' and he had tattoos up his arms right, an anchor here and a microwave here.
Pal: He didn't.
Kelly: He did. He said do you want a drink or do you want a kick up the bum with an open-toed sandal. I said get you Eamonn Andrews.
Pal: You didn't.
Kelly: I did. I said I'll have a pint of babycham, some pork scratchings and a yellow cherry and if I'm not here when you get back I'll be in t' toilet putting hide and heal on my love bites.
Pal: You didn't.
Kelly: I did. So I come out of the toilets, right, and he says hey scallop face your skirt's all caught up in your knickers at back, I said I pity you do you know why, he says why, I says 'cos it happens to be the latest fashion, I read it in a book, he says what book, I said *Vogue* that's what book, he said oh likely likely when do you read *Vogue*, I said when I'm in the hospital having exploratory surgery that's when. So he said oh.
Pal: He didn't.
Kelly: He did. And he sits there, right, picking the quiz off his beer-mat, and he says what were they exploring for, I said well it wasn't the Left Bank of the blinking Limpopo.

(Wood 1988: 121–2)

The humour here is in the bizarre detail – the man's microwave tattoo, Kelly's drink-order, and the relish of words and phrases like 'Limpopo' and 'exploratory surgery' – but also in the shape of the dialogue. Kelly's speech-rhythms mimic the rapid reported speech of gossip, with Wood – like Gertrude Stein – delighting in ordinary repetitions made strange: 'I said I pity you do you know why, he says why, I says . . .'. Her outrageous story is framed by a refrain also drawn from everyday conversation, but repeated for rhythmic effect, as the rush of Kelly's disclosures is halted by her friend's reaction and her own response to it, 'He did . . . I did . . . I was'. In performance, Wood's comic dialogues sound 'natural', but, like all good comedy, their language is carefully crafted and organised so that the funny ideas are delivered funnily.

ACTIVITY 4:

Assemble a collection of jokes, witticisms, and lines that have made you laugh, drawn from everyday speech or professional entertainment. If you are working in groups, perform them to each other or read them aloud to yourself. Try to decide which aspects of the language, phrasing, syntax and emphasis contribute to the comedy. What problems of speaking and performance do they raise? Summarise your conclusions in a short commentary.

Rhythm, voice and oral cultures

The deliberate foregrounding of rhythm is also a strategy used by writers who wish to deviate from the voice of Standard English. As we have seen, written and spoken languages are intimately connected – all prose has a 'voice' – and writers in English from Scotland, Africa, the Caribbean, India, and elsewhere have translated the local power of oral versions of English in these cultures to writing. Once again, it is the rhythm which is peculiar to a particular culture that defines the 'voice' of the prose.

The Trinidadian writer Earl Lovelace uses the distinctive inflections of his island's language in all his work. In this passage from the novel *Salt* (1996) the narrator gives an ironically sympathetic account of Trinidad's history of slavery and colonisation from the point of view of the colonisers:

Maybe that madness seized Columbus and the first set of conquerors when they land here and wanted the Carib people to believe that they was gods; but, afterwards, after they settle in the island and decide that, yes, is here we going to live now, they begin to discover how hard it was to be gods.

The heat, the diseases, the weight of armour they had to carry in the hot sun, the imperial poses they had to strike, the powdered wigs to wear, the churches to build, the heathen to baptize, the illiterates to educate, the animals to tame, the numerous species of plants to name, history to write, flags to plant, parades to make, the militia to assemble, letters to write home. And all around them, this rousing greenness bursting in the wet season and another quieter shade perspiring in the dry.

On top of that they had to put up with the noise from Blackpeople. Whole night Blackpeople have their drums going as they dance in the bush. All those dances. All those lascivious bodies leaping and bending down. They couldn't see them in the dark among the shadows and trees; but, they could hear. They had to listen to them dance the Bamboula Bamboula, the Quelbay, the Manding, the Juba, the Ibo, the Pique, the Halicord, the Coromanti, the Congo, the Chiffon, the Banda, the Pencow, the Cherrup, the Kalinda, the Bongo. It was hard for Whitepeople. It had days they wanted to just sit down under a breadfruit tree and cool off, to reach up and pick a ripe mango off the tree and eat it. It had times they just wanted to jump into the sea and take a sea bath, to romp with a girl on a bed of dead leaves underneath the umbrella of cocoa trees. They try, but they had it very hard. They walk a little distance and then they had to stop, perspiration soaking them, sticking their clothes to their bodies. It was so hot. They had to get these big roomy cork hats to wear to keep their brains cool. They had to get people to fan them. People to carry their swords, people to carry cushions for them to sit down on. They had to get people to beat people for them, people to dish out lashes – seventy-five, thirty-five, eighty-five. But, what else to do? People had to get licks to keep them in line. How else they coulda carry on The Work, feeding all those people, giving them rations, putting clothes on their back. And it was hard. It was very hard to mould the Negro character, to stamp out his savage tendencies.

(Lovelace 1996: 5–6)

The Trinidadian verb form in 'they was gods' in the first paragraph alerts us to the cultural identity of the narrator – this is not to be the supposedly 'neutral' (or strictly grammatically 'correct') voice of Standard English, but an account of conflict which recognises language as part of that conflict and as part of the complex inheritance of empire in the Caribbean. What follows is an imaginative evocation of the colonisers' lives in a prose that is an amalgam of English and Trinidadian, the interchange of languages pointing up the ironies and idiosyncrasies of colonial history. The long list of the burdens of empire in the second paragraph reflects the itemising instinct of mercantile invaders, and the length of the list perhaps mimics Caribbean 'shit-talk' (playful extravagance of language and invention). In the final sentence the longer, lyrical rhythms move from parodying the power of invasion to evoking the natural power of the land itself.

The third paragraph deals with the central moral issue of colonist–slave relations, entering the consciousness of the former whilst playfully supplying him with the speech-rhythms of the latter. 'Whole night Blackpeople have their drums going' is a slave-owner's complaint in the language of the slave, allowing Lovelace to express the fascination of the coloniser for the rhythms and actions over which he has no control, despite 'owning' the people who perform them. The list that follows returns us to the sequence of duties in the previous paragraph, but here the items are not weary necessities but dances, the names intruding an African patterning of sound. Instead of imposing himself on his slaves, the coloniser is shown enduring the culture that he has imported. His afflictions are further defined in the next section, which describes the colonists' temptations to indolence and sensuality, the syntax returning to the slower rhythms of the last sentence of the previous paragraph.

Irony and shit-talk's return is announced in the terse, mock-sympathy of 'They try, but they had it very hard', whereby the pity that is now normally reserved for the slave is transferred to their owners. It is a sentiment repeated after another list, this time of the violence committed on the Africans, but in the register and syntax of a racist empire: 'It was very hard to mould the Negro character, to stamp out his savage tendencies'. Playful variation of rhythm, language and their cultural meanings allows Lovelace to write about a painful historical subject and yet celebrate the resilience and comic resources of African-Caribbeans, setting off the oral freedoms of parody and mockery against the stiffness of the colonial lifestyle and its language of power.

ACTIVITY 5:

Examine the following extract from Zora Neale Hurston's novel *Their Eyes Were Watching God* (1937). Hurston, an African-American writer from Florida, describes her main character, Janie, returning to her village, also in northern Florida. What rhythmic effects does Hurston achieve and how? Why might she be writing in this way? Summarise your observations in a short commentary.

The people all saw her come because it was sundown. The sun was gone, but he had left his footprints in the sky. It was the time for sitting on porches beside the road. It was the time to hear things and talk. These sitters had been tongueless, earless, eyeless conveniences all day long. Mules and other brutes had occupied their skins. But now, the sun and the bossman were gone, so the skins felt powerful and human. They became lords of sounds and lesser things. They passed nations through their mouths. They sat in judgement.

Seeing the woman as she was made them remember the envy they had stored up from other times. So they chewed up the back parts of their minds and swallowed with relish. They made burning statements with questions, and killing tools out of laughs. It was mass cruelty. A mood come alive. Words walking without masters; walking altogether like harmony in a song.

'What she doin' coming back here in dem overhalls? Can't she find no dress to put on? – Where's dat blue satin dress she left here in? – Where all dat money her husband took and died and left her? – What dat ole forty year ole 'oman doin' wid her hair swingin' down her back lak some young gal? – Where she left dat young lad of a boy she went off here wid? – Thought she was going to marry? – Where he left *her*? – What he done wid all her money? – Betcha he off wid some gal so young she ain't even got no hairs – why she don't stay in her class? –'

When she got to where they were she turned her face on the bander log and spoke. They scrambled a noisy 'good evenin'' and left their mouths setting open and their ears full of hope. Her speech was pleasant enough, but she kept walking straight on to her gate. The porch couldn't talk for looking.

(Hurston 1986: 9–10)

Rhythm and voice in non-literary writing

So far we have been looking at the ways writers of fiction, drama and comedy have used rhythmic effects. But other kinds of writing – technical, critical, and general communication – also have a voice, and the best practitioners of them understand the value of rhythmic variation and emphasis. Advertisers have long exploited this to shape striking phrases that embed themselves in the often unwilling minds of passers-by and casual listeners. The instructions on my bank's cashpoint machine once had a striking rhythmic pattern that, intentionally or not, made me remember it ('Remove your card then take your money'). My head is full of more or less irritating advertising sentences, some of them from thirty years ago: 'Hot Chocolate Drinking Chocolate', 'That's the Wonder of Woolworth'. Try as I might to get rid of them, their rhythms keep them there.

ACTIVITY 6:

Find two or three examples of the effective and inventive use of rhythm in advertising or other public uses of language. Add a few lines of commentary saying why you think it is effective and memorable.

Even in everyday prose, such as business correspondence, the rule of 'reason persuades but rhythm convinces' still holds good. The following letter, from a restaurant owner, is a complaint directed against a disruptive customer:

Dear Mr Callaghan,
 A member of your party which lunched with us yesterday made an unparalleled scene at our restaurant. His exhibition of hectoring rudeness left two of my staff in tears, and gave them no chance whatever of responding to his – thoroughly unreasonable – complaints. Had he allowed them to do so, they would certainly have done their utmost to satisfy him, however unjustified his remarks and uncouth his method of expressing them.
 If your friend is in the habit of making public attacks upon people whom, he may feel, are in a poor position to defend themselves, it is perhaps less than fair to inflict him on restaurants and their customers. Mr Callaghan said he would not be coming to eat with us again. You may assure him that we would never knowingly accept his custom in the future. I would be most grateful if you would pass on the enclosed cheque, being the sum Mr Callaghan so grudgingly paid. We have no need, nor intention, of profiting from such a personality.
 Yours faithfully etc.,

The intention of this piece of controlled invective is both to reinforce the restaurant's codes of behaviour and to ensure that the customer realises the unacceptability of his friend's behaviour. The letter is cogently argued and structured, outlining the context, stating how the complaint could have been made and the restaurant staff's willingness to deal with it, before banning Mr Callaghan and refusing to take his money. What makes it a devastatingly effective letter, however, is the control of its syntax and its rhythmic force. The writer is obviously angry, but the anger is conveyed through a generally understated register ('unjustified', 'uncouth', '[y]ou may assure') contrasted with the occasional use of less diplomatic language ('hectoring rudeness', 'grudgingly paid', and the final reduction of Mr Callaghan to a 'personality'). This mixture of registers is contained within the restraints of relatively complex syntax (anger normally simplifies grammar), until the middle of the third paragraph where the ban on Mr Callaghan is announced in two noticeably shorter sentences, the break in rhythm emphasising the action, before the letter closes with the over-polite request to return the money. Without ever resorting to abuse – Mr Callaghan's territory, evidently – the letter uses the full force of controlled rhythm, syntax and register to deliver a telling response.

If business correspondence is an unlikely source of rhythmic prose, then so is critical writing. Criticism sometimes has the reputation for dullness of expression, as if to write about art and culture demands the repression of the most interesting features of language. This is not always the case, however. Here is Nick Tosches writing about that most difficult of subjects, music. He examines the effect of Jerry Lee Lewis's rock-and-roll record 'Whole Lotta Shakin' Goin' On' in *Hellfire: The Jerry Lee Lewis Story* (1982):

> Fame lifted her skirt for the final wild son. As the summer passed, hot Southern day upon hot Southern night, the sound of 'Whole Lotta Shakin' Goin' On' grew louder and more ominous. It was everywhere, blasting forth like thunder without rain from cars and bars and all the open windows of the unsaved. Its wicked rhythm devoured the young of the land. It bloodied virgins and stirred new housewives to recall things they never spoke of. It inspired boys to reinvent themselves as flaming new creatures and to seek detumescence without ruth.
>
> By the end of July, 'Whole Lotta Shakin' Goin' On' had sold about 100,000 copies. Then it ran into trouble. Many people feared the song and its singer. Even some who liked Elvis damned Jerry Lee as lascivious and evil. Mothers smelled his awful presence in the laundry of their daughters, and preachers stood before their flocks and railed against him and his sinful song. Slowly, radio stations began to ban the record, and it was heard less and less.

(Tosches 1982: 125–6)

Tosches' piece solves the problem of writing an account of exciting music by mingling the informative with a kind of prose that draws on the extravagance of the music itself and its sources in the emotional Baptist churches of the American South. The long, heavily-accented syntax and rhetorical register of the Authorised Version of the Bible are used in unlikely conjunction with the language and life of 1950s teenagers, as in the evocation of divine wrath 'blasting forth like thunder without rain' conjoined with the archetypal locations of rock and roll, 'cars and bars'. Likewise, the emergence of teenage sexuality is converted into the image and cadence of apocalyptic revelation as Jerry Lee's music stalks the land like a pestilence bloodying virgins and scenting laundry. Amongst these ironic hyperboles, Tosches supplies prosaic information about record sales and social attitudes, though once again with an awareness of the need for rhythmic variation, as demonstrated by the contrasting length of the first and second sentences of the second paragraph.

Less extravagant than Tosches, but still with a keen sense of the need to make commentary sensuously as well as intellectually interesting to a reader, is the critic Kenneth Tynan. In the following passage he is describing a performance of Bertolt Brecht's play *Mother Courage and Her Children*:

> As the tireless old protagonist, dragging her canteen wagon across the battlefields of the Thirty Years' War, Helene Weigel played in a manner that shrank utterly from flamboyance; her performance was graphic yet casual, like a shrug. At two carefully selected moments she was piercingly and unforgettably moving – first in the soundless cry that doubles her up when her son is executed, and again when, to avoid incriminating herself, she must pretend not to recognise his body. She walks over to the stretcher, wearing a feigned, frozen smile that does not budge from her lips until she has surveyed the corpse, shaken her head, and returned to her seat on the other side of the stage. Then she turns to the audience, and we see for an instant the drained, stone face of absolute grief.

(Tynan 1989: 136)

Tynan is trying to convey both the method of Helene Weigel's performance as Mother Courage and the special quality of particular moments of theatre. He chooses to write in long, fairly complex sentences, and each is modulated for specific effects. In the first sentence, the main clause is delayed, the delay mirroring the relentlessness of the action of the play. After the semi-colon, the short final phrase, 'like a shrug', again seems to mirror the performance, the clause being used almost as an afterthought in the sentence. The shorter final sentence, ending emphatically with 'absolute grief', allows the reader a sense of the shock of performance. Tynan leads us through the emotion and drama of the scene by varying the rhythms of his account.

ACTIVITY 7:

Select some examples of business or critical prose that seem to you interesting (or uninteresting) in their approach to language – you might consider newspaper and magazine reviews of music, theatre, cinema and books, and circular letters from banks, insurance companies, and any kind of 'formal' correspondence. Which aspects of their prose styles are effective? What improvements to the rhythmic interest of the writing could you make?

Rhythm and voice in academic writing

Academic writing is rarely as stylised or rhetorically inventive as that of Tosches and Tynan, but the lessons of their experimental and thoughtful use of the patterns of language to keep the reader interested and give him or her a sense of the excitement of reading and ideas are useful ones. A good essay communicates enthusiasm and enthusiasm expresses itself in rhythm.

We can consider these points in two example paragraphs from under-graduate essays on the work of African-American novelist Zora Neale Hurston (an extract from her novel *Their Eyes Were Watching God* was included above).

Essay 1

The storytelling sessions on the porch, first in Eatonville and then in the Everglades, clearly functioned as a bonding force of the community. They provided people with a reason to meet up and socialize. The telling of stories is a form of entertainment in the communities Hurston describes, but their subject matter suggests that they have been invented not merely to entertain, but also to explain. Many of the stories in *Mules and Men* deal with slavery, and with the situation of the black population, and it seems likely that these stories have been told in an attempt to deal with the situation in which the oppressed black people found themselves. The storytelling is a way of achieving some distance from the hardships of everyday life. After a long day of working like mules, the workers can retire to tell stories about mules, to become 'lords of sounds' rather than the 'tongueless, earless, eyeless conveniences' they have been all day. This creates a space of freedom and a place of power. To be a teller of stories is to be powerful.

Essay 2

Janie [the main character in *Their Eyes Were Watching God*] finally recognises the power of language and she uses it to assert her individuality: 'But Ah'm uh woman every inch of me, and I know it . . . You big-bellies round here . . . 'taint nothin to it but yo' big voice . . . When you pull down yo' britches, you look lak de change uh life.' This can be described as an example of role-reversal, as Janie uses language to assert her femininity and destroy the illusion of Joe's [her husband's] masculinity. It is significant that, due to Janie using language in an assertive manner, Joe is lost for words: 'Joe Starks didn't know the word for this . . . so he struck Janie with all his might'. Joe associates the use of language with power, and as Janie has verbally defeated him, he believes that he can only assert his authority through violence. Soon after this verbal defeat, Joe dies; one could argue that, due to the power of language, Janie has killed him by destroying his public persona. Janie considers Joe's death as liberating, and this is shown in the manner in which she tells the community of his death: '[she] opened up the window and cried, "Come heah people! Jody is dead. Mah husband is gone from me"'. The fact that she chooses to tell the community by *crying* indicates that she is excited by it.

ACTIVITY 8:

Read these paragraphs aloud. Which do you think is better? Write a short commentary addressed to the student whose handling of prose rhythms you think could be improved, outlining some of the practical changes s/he could make to improve the effectiveness of the writing.

Both passages make interesting and informed points about the relationship of language and power in Hurston's novel. But while the second essay would pass reasonably, the first would pass well, and this has little to do with what the two writers know and think about Hurston, but almost everything to do with the way they express their knowledge and opinions.

The first paragraph begins with a crisp topic sentence, outlining simply the point the section will make. Subsequent sentences vary in length and structure, the simple second sentence contrasting with the longer third, which balances statement and qualification. Later the writer adroitly varies the rhythm of her writing by introducing direct quotation from Hurston's prose, before capping the paragraph with two short sentences, the second of which makes a simple and effective summary of the main point. The writer of the second essay also sees the value of quotation, but introduces it clumsily so that the rhythms of black American vernacular break up rather than enhance those of the essay. And the rhythms of the essay are themselves uncertain, with each sentence tending to use the same syntactic pattern and forming isolated and monotonous units. The information contained in these units is sound and the points are interesting, but the faltering rhythms of the prose point up the lack of a sure sense of a developing argument.

ACTIVITY 9:

Take the second of the essay extracts and, without altering the content of the piece significantly, rework the syntax and punctuation to make it more rhythmically effective. Try out several drafts until you are happy with the final rhythmic patterns of the piece. Add a few sentences explaining how you have improved it.

ACTIVITY 10:

Choose an extract from your own recent academic writing. Analyse its prose and assess its effectiveness and interest in terms of its rhythmic variety and emphasis. Are there any ways in which you can apply the techniques discussed in this chapter to your own prose style? Rewrite the extract and add a few sentences explaining how you think you have improved it.

Rhythm convinces. In whatever form of writing we are reading or composing, the voice of the piece and its rhythms control the effectiveness of the expression, and, whether they know it or not, readers are influenced by the patterns of language that they hear in their head.

Summary

In this chapter we have looked at:

- the importance of rhythm in the creation of fictional voices
- the relationship between the rhythms of prose and the rhythms of the speaking voice
- the use of rhythm to elicit specific responses such as laughter
- the expression of cultural differences through rhythmic effects
- the importance of rhythm in non-fictional, critical and academic writing.

References

Coetzee, J.M. (1982) *In the Heart of the Country* [1977]. Harmondsworth: Penguin.
Hurston, Zora Neale (1986) *Their Eyes Were Watching God* [1937]. London: Virago.
Lovelace, Earl (1996) *Salt*. London: Faber.
Pinter, Harold (1978) *The Homecoming* [1964] in *Plays: Three*. London: Eyre Methuen.
Poe, Edgar Allen (1978) *Tales of Mystery and Imagination* [1845]. London: Dent.
Stein, Gertrude (1968) *Geography and Plays* [1922]. New York: Something Else Press.
Tosches, Nick (1982) *Hellfire: The Jerry Lee Lewis Story*. London: Plexus.
Tynan, Kenneth (1989) *Profiles*. London: Nick Hern Books.
Wood, Victoria (1988) *Barmy*. London: Methuen.

CHAPTER 6

Styles of journalism

Dominic Rowland and Simon Avery

In the course of this book we have examined a range of techniques and approaches designed to help you develop your skills both in stylistic analysis and effective writing. We have focused upon the appropriate choice of diction, register and rhythm, as well as the need for careful structuring and the importance of being aware of the audience for whom the text is produced. These elements have been examined in a wide range of texts drawn from different contexts, cultures and historical periods, and have included literary fiction, drama, advertising, academic essays and more business-orientated documents. This means that you should now possess a keener sense of the varieties of writing to be found around us and an understanding of the means by which such writings achieve their effects.

In this final chapter we're going to draw upon many of the ideas we have explored previously and use them in relation to a particular case study – the styles of writing to be found in journalism. We've chosen journalism because the genre contains so much stylistic variety (editorials, reviews, feature articles, polemical writing, analytical writing, description and so on), and in addition to improving your analytical skills further, we will use this variety to offer some more general tips for effective writing.

The main part of this chapter will focus on writing for newspapers and will consider journalistic language, the construction of headlines, the structuring of an article, bias and objectivity, the need for clarity, and the processes of redrafting and editing. The final sections of the chapter will then build on these and other elements by examining writing for magazines and the range of styles to be found there. Overall, then, this chapter should help you consolidate much of what you have already learnt and give you a sound understanding of the varieties of journalism.

Before continuing you should make sure that you have some recent newspapers to hand, as several of the exercises will ask you to work on your own examples of journalistic writing. Try to get a mix of newspapers so that you can contrast the different reporting styles. In Britain, unlike in the United States for instance, there is a sizeable number of national large-circulation newspapers, which can be divided into three distinct groups: the *broadsheets*, which are sometimes pejoratively called 'the heavies' (*The Daily Telegraph, The Financial Times, The Guardian, The Independent* and *The Times*); the *mid-market tabloids* (*The Daily Express* and *The Daily Mail*); and the *mass-market tabloids* (*The Mirror, The Star* and *The Sun*). When making your selection of papers, try to choose at least one broadsheet and one tabloid, and perhaps also a local newspaper. You will also need a number of magazines for use in the later parts of this chapter. Again, try to choose a variety which will reflect different interests – remember, the wider your choice of material, the more diverse will be the range of styles on which you will be able to work.

Newspaper layouts

Journalism is one of the most common varieties of writing we encounter and most people read it several times during any particular week – in press releases, corporate publications and magazines, as well as in newspapers. In this part of the chapter we will be studying news journalism as a distinct variety of language use, but we must remember that within the covers of any particular newspaper there are many different types of prose, all of which are adapted for different uses. Some provide information about local, regional, national and international events in what are commonly called *news stories*, while others attempt to persuade readers of the author's particular views on various issues in articles called *comment, opinion* or *leaders*. Conventionally, news material and opinion material are kept distinct and separate, but as we will see, this distinction is often blurred in practice and the way in which the news is reported can clearly influence the opinions readers form about it. Other newspaper pieces might be biographical in nature or provide instruction or advice about gardening, DIY or cooking, for instance. Each of these varieties of writing is likely to have its own house style and it's important that we are aware of them – as we have seen throughout this book, the style of a piece always has an influence on the ways in which we read and respond to it.

Although newspapers are increasingly diverse in the information they contain, then, they are basically made up of articles. In the broadsheet newspapers, articles on the same basic subject (home news, international news, politics – what others can you think of?) are grouped together in an order which varies little from day to day and which therefore gives the newspaper structure and identity. A regular reader of *The Guardian*, for example, will get used to the usual layout and article groupings and will expect the International News section to follow the National News section, and the Sports section to follow the Finance section. Take a few minutes to look through one of the newspapers you have collected. Is there any patterning to be found in the way the articles are put together? What are the effects of this patterning?

Of course, one feature whose positioning is the same in all types of newspaper is the lead story on the front page. It is crucial that this story grabs the attention of the potential reader if the paper is to sell as many copies as possible. Remember, of course, that newspapers are commercial ventures and participate in a highly competitive field, and so much is resting on the effectiveness of the lead story. It doesn't necessarily have to be the most important or 'newsworthy' piece (although it often is), but something which the editor believes will draw readers to buy that particular paper rather than another.

The tabloids often devote the vast majority, if not all, of the front page to one lead story, which may also be accompanied by a large headline and a photograph. In contrast, the broadsheets usually have more than one story on the front page, along with photographs, so that the main story has to be emphasised in other ways. It may, for example, appear in the top left-hand corner of the page, the dominant position to which the eye is usually drawn, or its headline may use larger or bolder type than those of other stories. The length of the story and the amount of space it occupies on the page is obviously another guide to how important the editor considers it to be.

In addition to the verbal content of an article, therefore, the way in which it is *presented* on the page affects our experience of reading and the information or judgements which we, as readers, take away with us. We can divide the main elements which are regularly employed in the presentation of newspaper articles into two broad categories:

- graphological factors such as page layout (spacing, length of paragraphs, etc.), use of photographs (sometimes a headline cannot be understood without its accompanying photograph), and other visual images – cartoons, charts, maps, graphs, the ratio of content to advertising material, etc.
- typographical factors such as type size variation, and the use of bold, italics, capitals, underlining, and different fonts.

ACTIVITY 1:

Choose two or three front pages from the newspapers you have collected and assess what factors have been used in order to attract the attention of a potential reader. What is the relationship between the text and photograph (if there is one)? What is the effect of any graphological or typographical features used? If you are working in a group, compare your ideas with those of the other group members. Then write a couple of paragraphs comparing the effectiveness of the front pages you have chosen. Is there anything you think could be done better?

Now choose a piece of your own writing – it might be a piece you have produced while working through this book or something else. Consider if there are any places where typographical and/or graphological elements could be used to effect. Again, think carefully about the relationship between content and presentation.

Audience

All forms of journalism are varieties of writing which emphasise both clear communication (most readers expect to be able to read an article fairly quickly) and information (readers want newspapers to tell them something they don't already know). As we have emphasised throughout this book, you must always bear in mind your audience when you write, as this can affect a whole host of elements such as word choice, sentence structure, tone, etc. So, for example, the legal document, tourist brochure and thank-you note which we looked at in the section on register in Chapter 2 all employ language and syntactical structures which are suitable for their particular audiences (lawyers, potential holiday-makers and a close friend). Journalism is no exception to this rule of 'know your audience'. In fact, a knowledge and understanding of the potential readership is absolutely crucial if journalists are to keep their readers buying the paper day after day. Editors and journalists are therefore constantly attempting to build up trust, familiarity and loyalty in their readers. In the broadsheets such loyalty is usually only implied, but articles in the mass-market tabloids frequently make reference to the supposed relationship between the newspaper and its readers. A paper such as *The Daily Mail* or *The Sun*, therefore, might refer to its 'loyal army of readers', indicating its large and dedicated following. Such loyalty among readers of a particular paper will result in part from the belief that the paper's reports and stories contain a high degree of accuracy (although, of course, this isn't always the case!), but equally important is the way in which a reader often chooses a newspaper because it shares his or her own attitudes, views and beliefs, and reports the news in such as way as to reflect these. (We'll return to this point in the section 'Slanting and bias' below.)

ACTIVITY 2:

In the newspapers you have collected, try to find examples of the ways in which journalists and editors refer to their readers. Is there a difference between the way the tabloids do this and the way the broadsheets do it? What does this imply about the assumed reader/writer relationships? How effective are the methods? If you are working in a group, discuss your opinions with the other group members. Then write up your observations as a short report.

Having considered the ways in which the reader is addressed in newspaper articles, do you think it would be appropriate to use any of these techniques in your own academic work or in any other types of writing you produce? If so, where and how would you use them?

The language of headlines

As we have examined throughout this book, many types of writing have their own particular language styles, and journalism is no exception. The distinct language of newspapers is called *journalese*, of which *tabloidese* is a variant (you might like to look at Keith Waterhouse's 1993 book *Waterhouse on Newspaper Style* for a humorous discussion of the characteristics of these styles). Of course, journalese is often very different from the language that we use in everyday conversation. *The Sun* might label its editorial 'THE SUN SAYS', for example, as if its writing is a speech act and therefore more immediate, but it is unlikely that anyone ever really speaks like a tabloid.

Newspaper articles begin with headlines and this is a good place for us to start thinking about how journalists manipulate language to create specific effects. Typically, headlines should attract the reader's attention and therefore they often use words and phrases which are punchy, startling, or which leave the reader wanting to read on. They usually indicate the article's subject matter and might also act as a summary of it, as in 'Worcester Building Society Sold in Private Deal' or 'Martians Took My Brother'. One of the most famous, indeed infamous, headlines of recent times was the one word 'GOTCHA!' which appeared in six-inch-high bold capitals on the front page of *The Sun* on 4 May 1982, during the Falklands conflict. The word is a neologism – that is, a newly coined word – which is a colloquial contraction of the phrase 'I/We have got you'. The spelling functions as a direct transliteration of the colloquial pronunciation, making it an extremely active and dynamic word. The notoriety of the headline arises out of its particular reference to the sinking of the *Belgrano*, an Argentine warship. The headline suggests that the newspaper itself (and by extension its presumably fiercely patriotic readers) had some hand in the military victory, but such triumphalism seems particularly tasteless given the large number of Argentines who were killed.

What this example demonstrates, however, is the way in which headlines attempt to achieve maximum verbal economy and impact. They often do this by employing a range of linguistic devices, including alliteration, assonance, rhyme, puns, homonyms, homophones, idioms, colloquial phrases and emotive words. Take a few minutes to check you understand these terms by filling in the table below. Your examples can be drawn from any kind of text – we will see how these techniques are used specifically in headlines in a moment. Remember, if there are any terms that you're unsure about, you can check them in a dictionary or the glossary at the back of this book.

ACTIVITY 3:

Complete the table below.

Term	Definition	Example
alliteration		
assonance		
rhyme		
pun		
homonym		
homophone		
idiom		
colloquial phrase		
emotive word		

Let's now take a look at some headlines and see how these linguistic devices are used. In the headline 'Farmhouse Fire Fury', for example, a story about how a sacked farm employee burnt down his employer's home, the effect is achieved through alliteration across all three words. The headline 'Children Drawn into Hellevision', which introduces a story about the detrimental effects of children having access to 'video nasties', achieves its effects through the obvious rhyme with television. The headline for a story about a road-sweeper who was imprisoned for theft from his employer, 'Brush with the Law', works by investing a commonly used phrase with extra significance – the brush is obviously an allusion to the road-sweeper's occupation. And the headline 'Room with a Queue', a story about a couple's disastrous honeymoon when they find their hotel suite has been booked for two other couples at the same time, uses a cultural reference to, and pun upon, the title of E.M. Forster's famous novel *A Room with a View*. We've made up these examples but they demonstrate how the effects of headlines are often achieved through such forms of wordplay.

Another common device in the construction of headlines is the use of *noun phrases*. A noun phrase is a group of words made up of a main noun (the head or essential word) accompanied by added information in the form of words called *modifiers*. *Pre-modifiers* come before the head noun and *post-modifiers* follow it. In headlines, pre-modification is used more frequently than post-modification as a way of packing more information into the minimum of space. The headlines 'Deserted Rebel Village' and 'Doctor's Mercy Killings', for example, both use pre-modified noun phrases. Sometimes pre-modification is used to generate suspense in the reader, giving the headline dramatic effect (as in the examples above), while at other times it is used simply as a form of name-tagging or conventional labelling, as in 'footie-star fiancé David Beckham' or 'hard-hitting interviewer Jeremy Paxman'. (For more information on noun phrases and modification see the first book in this series, *Grammar and Writing*.)

ACTIVITY 4:

Choose five headlines from your newspapers and analyse the linguistic effects which they employ (alliteration, puns, pre-modification, etc.). Then carefully read the articles they introduce and come up with your own, alternative headlines. Write a sentence accompanying each one explaining how your headlines are constructed.

Structure and style

As we've emphasised throughout this book, careful structuring is essential with any piece of writing, of whatever length or subject matter and for whomever it is written. Whether you're writing a novel, a letter to a friend, or a recipe, clear structuring is the key to effective communication. In writing their copy (material for an article), journalists are similarly faced with a range of issues about structure. The piece must be interesting to the readers (if possible, interesting enough that they will read to the end of it) and so it must engage them from the beginning. It must justify its inclusion in the paper by finding an angle that makes it newsworthy. And it must also be clear and readable and comprehensible without reference to external sources. All these considerations influence the structuring. Let's start by looking at the following example which, although a relatively simple piece invented by us, is typical of the short human interest pieces often found in local newspapers.

PURR-FECT ENDING

Tigger, a beloved tabby cat lost by distraught granny Mary Bentley of Green Street, was returned home safe and sound yesterday – after spending three weeks at a house two streets away!

Mary's feline friend and only companion had disappeared one evening and Mary feared that she would never see him again.

But Jenny Campbell, 68, found Tigger scratching at her door and, thinking he was a stray, took him in where he subsequently stayed.

Jenny did not know Mary but three weeks later she heard someone talking about the missing cat and realised what had happened.

Tearful Mary said yesterday: 'I'm overjoyed to get Tigger back and I'm so grateful to Jenny for looking after him so well.'

Although this is obviously a very thin piece in terms of news value – as such accounts often are – we can use it to make some more general points about the structuring of journalistic narratives. The opening sentence (often called the *lead*) is used here to summarise the story and to capture the readers' attention so that they will want to read on to discover more. Leads often attempt to create suspense or surprise, or shock or arouse emotions in the reader. The first sentence here also has the effect of chronologically restructuring the report, so that we are told of the happy resolution at the beginning. The preceding drama is then unfolded in the subsequent paragraphs, each of which deals with a specific event, before the reader is taken back to the owner's happiness in the final paragraph. Stylistically, there's a strong preference for sentences which are either simple statements or co-ordinated (joining two statements together using 'and' or 'but'). There's little use of complex sentences with multiple clauses as these would impede the immediacy which the journalist wishes to achieve. (For more information on these sentence types, see the first book in this series, *Grammar and Writing*.) The diction (vocabulary) is also clear and accessible, which makes it suitable for a wide readership, and we are drawn into what is otherwise a fairly dull account by the emphasis on the emotional importance of the cat's return – Tigger is Mary's 'only companion' and she is 'distraught' at his loss. Such emotionally loaded language is typical of pieces like this.

Another striking aspect of newspaper style, in comparison with fiction for instance, is the very high ratio of paragraphs to sentences. In the story of Tigger's escapades printed above, for example, the ratio is 1:1. This is a style which is also often found in more serious, political reporting. Here, for example, are the opening paragraphs of an article on the Foreign Secretary Robin Cook's alleged involvement with arms trading:

Robin Cook was yesterday cleared by an inquiry into the arms-to-Africa affair.

An independent report found that the Foreign Secretary and his ministers had no knowledge of the illegal supply of weapons to Sierra Leone.

But the probe by former civil servant Sir Thomas Legg severely criticised Foreign Office officials' handling of the affair.

And Mr Cook yesterday vowed to make sweeping changes to his department in the wake of the crisis.

(*The Mirror*, 28 June 1998: 8)

Such short paragraphs would certainly be inappropriate in many other forms of writing. Rather than representing a unit of *thought* – the main purpose of a paragraph in an essay – the paragraphs in journalism are often used simply as units of *length*, breaking the information down to the smallest units which are easily digestible by the reader. As a result, journalists often rely heavily on conjunctions (linking words) to create a sense of flow from paragraph to paragraph. In the section from the Robin Cook article quoted above, for example, two of the paragraphs begin with conjunctions ('But', 'And'). Take a few minutes now to look at a piece of your own writing. How many sentences do you use in a paragraph on average? What is the effect of this and how does it differ from journalistic writing?

Let's now turn to the structuring and stylistic techniques used in a longer piece of journalism. The passage below comes from a news report about a woman who fell into a coma for three months due to a viral condition commonly known as 'sleeping sickness'.

[1]   When Becky Howells had shooting pains across her forehead, she took two paracetamol and went to bed.

[2]   The lively 23-year-old thought her headache would go by morning. But when she awoke Becky was surrounded by her worried parents and brother in a strange room with a tangle of wires and tubes attached to her.

[3]   It was Christmas Eve. Becky was in hospital and had been asleep for THREE MONTHS.

[4]   Five years on her case still baffles doctors, who do not know if the condition will strike again.

[5]   Her experiences will feature in a television documentary on the mysterious illness encephalitis lethargica or sleeping sickness that swept Europe in the 1920s.

[6]   The virus, which causes inflammation of the brain, killed one million and left thousands in a deep sleep from which they never awoke.

[7]   Hundreds more victims were frozen like statues, prisoners in their own bodies until death.

[8]   The bug, the basis for the Hollywood film *Awakenings*, virtually disappeared in 1928 as quickly as it arrived.

[9]   But another victim, Philip Leather, 77, is still 'asleep' in a psychiatric unit in Birmingham – 63 years after he was affected.

[10]   His was a unique case until office worker Becky fell ill.

(*The Mirror*, 28 July 1998: 15)

How can we analyse the structure and style of this piece? Again, it's a human interest story, but one which engages the reader because of the sheer suddenness with which Becky Howells is struck down and the sense that this could happen to any of us. In this case, it is the headline – which refers to the three-month long sleep – rather than the lead sentence which causes us to read on. Indeed, the first sentence is rather mundane, seeming to refer to an everyday occurrence which the protagonist imagines will be cleared by tablets and a good night's sleep. It's not until the third sentence (paragraph 2) that we are really gripped. The emphasis on 'But' as the first word of this sentence signals a change of narrative direction as we experience Becky's waking up in an alien environment, from her perspective. The main purpose of this sentence is therefore to create suspense before the next paragraph (3) hits us with the shocking truth that she has been unconscious for three months (emphasised by the use of capitals). The first sentence of this paragraph, 'It was Christmas Eve', adds to the drama both through the brevity of its length and the reference to a time of the year which is highly emotive and typically associated with families coming together for celebration. Such seasonal expectations are clearly at odds with Becky's situation. At the start of paragraph 4, a time transition phrase ('Five years on') takes us up to the present day, but only to increase the sense of anxiety as we, like the doctors, don't know if or when the illness will reoccur (the verb 'strike' here suggests the rapidity with which it might do so).

   After these introductory four paragraphs there is a shift from narrative style (the recounting of the story) to a more *expository* style. Exposition is the prose of informing or explaining and the next four paragraphs (5–8) give us factual information about the viral infection encephalitic lethargica (sleeping sickness) from which Becky suffers. Yet amidst the historical and medical facts contained here, there are also some blatant attempts to sensationalise the event. The vague numbers used to estimate the sufferers – 'thousands', 'hundreds' – add impact if not precision to the story, while the vivid construction of the victims as 'frozen . . . statues' and 'prisoners in their own bodies' almost suggests a scenario out of a horror film. The journalist also tries to make the condition more accessible by making a cultural reference (allusion) to the representation of the illness in the successful film *Awakenings*.

In the final paragraphs, there is another change of direction as we return from the emphasis on the general condition to the specifics of certain individuals – firstly a sufferer who has spent most of his life with this condition, and then back to Becky, returning us in circular fashion to the main focus of the article.

Again, as with Tigger's story, there is a preference in this piece for simple sentence types with which to achieve immediacy, and language which is accessible. Where a term is introduced which the reader might never have heard of (such as encephalitis lethargica), it is explained in everyday language ('sleeping sickness'). This is a point which is useful to remember for your own writing. As we suggested in Chapter 3, be careful of assuming that your readers understand the terminology which you might take for granted.

What this analysis demonstrates, then, is the way in which newspaper articles are carefully structured and use a range of stylistic techniques in order to gain the reader's attention and involvement. As we have seen throughout this book, such principles are crucial to any piece of writing if it is to communicate effectively.

ACTIVITY 5:

Choose an article from a newspaper and examine its structure and style in the way we did with the story above. It need not be a human interest story – a political story or current affairs article will work just as well. Make a list of points about the piece and then, if you are working in a group, discuss them with the other group members. Write up your analysis as a short report.

Keeping it concise

We have already discussed how headlines attempt to achieve maximum impact within a severely limited space, but space is at a premium in *all* journalism, of course, where the overall length of an article is particularly short in relation to other varieties of writing such as the essay or novel. Being concise is therefore crucial and before an article is sent to press it will be drafted and redrafted by the journalist and the sub-editor so that it conveys as much as possible in as few words as possible. What cannot be conveyed directly, therefore, will be connoted or implied in an attempt to enhance the news-value to the greatest extent. As with all well-crafted writing, verbal economy is not necessarily the same as semantic economy.

In Chapters 3 and 4 we examined a variety of editing techniques, many of which apply equally to journalistic writing. In particular, though, handbooks written to help journalists produce effective copy give the following points of advice:

- Aim for clarity and coherence.
- Keep focused and avoid waffle.
- Avoid tautology – using several words which mean the same thing (e.g. 'In my opinion, I think that', 'a pair of twins', 'razed to the ground').
- Avoid words which are old fashioned (archaic) or hackneyed, foreign expressions (e.g. 'demi-monde'), and mixed metaphors.
- Avoid repeating the same pieces of information over and again. Using a range of synonyms in an attempt to disguise the repetition is quite a common practice in newspapers, particularly where a journalist has to pad out an otherwise rather thin story. (The novelist Rebecca West once rather archly defined journalism as 'an ability to meet the challenge of filling the space'!);
- Use short words rather than long ones, and Anglo-Saxon words rather than Latinate ones. (This applies to tabloids in particular.) Monosyllables are often used for dramatic impact and are far more likely to be onomatopoeic. How often have you seen the word 'rap' used rather than its equivalent 'reprimand', 'slam' instead of 'criticise', and 'axed' instead of 'made redundant'? Such word choices are not just space-saving but are characteristic of the exuberant and dynamic lexicon of tabloidese.

ACTIVITY 6:

Choose a longish article from one of your papers. Imagine you are a sub-editor and you've been given this article by your editor. Space for copy is tighter than expected and you've been asked to edit the article and reduce it to half the number of words. Start by reading the piece through carefully. If you are working individually, make a list of changes you want to make and why. If you are working in a group, discuss what should be cut with the other group members. It's likely that you'll have different views, so try to come to some sort of consensus.

Then write your first version of the revised piece, attempting to reduce the number of words while keeping the salient points of the original. Then write a second draft where you attempt to polish what you have written and achieve maximum impact. Has the story been told in the best way it can? Is it ordered effectively? Is the language sharp and precise? Is the whole tightly written?

Slanting and bias in news reporting

In addition to distinguishing newspapers as tabloids or broadsheets, it is possible to classify them according to their political allegiances. For example,

The Guardian tends to favour a more left-wing bias, while *The Telegraph* tends to express a move right-wing viewpoint. Theoretically, a paper's affiliation to a particular political party or ideology should not affect how a news story is reported – news is news is news and a news story should simply record what happened. In practice, however, it is extremely unlikely that we will ever read something which is not influenced by ideological preference or bias. All newspapers will emphasis one angle over another and more often than not they won't acknowledge their partiality. Certain elements of a story will be silently selected and foregrounded while others will not, in order to give a report a particular focus. The slang term for this is 'putting a spin' on the news. Someone from outside the newspaper who influences the way that journalists report the news is a 'spin-doctor', while within the newspaper and its parent publishing company, the proprietor and editor may also be exercising forms of censorship which are often difficult to detect. So let's look at some news reports and see if we can identify the biases underlying them. This first piece is taken from *The Sun* and reports on a government statement about refugees.

> MIGRANT CON IS KOd Thousands of bogus refugees will be booted out of Britain under new rules pledged yesterday.
>
> Home Secretary Jack Straw promised to introduce a 'faster, fairer and firmer' immigration system. He aims to cut processing time for applications to two months to clear a 75,000 backlog. But he promised genuine asylum seekers would not suffer in his purge on the phonies, who cost tax-payers £12 million every week.
>
> (*The Sun*, 28 July 1998)

The most important and resonant term in the headline here is the word 'con', which sets the tone of the piece by suggesting that asylum-seeking in Britain is essentially a confidence trick. This belief is reinforced in the lead sentence through the adjective 'bogus' (emphasised through alliteration with 'booted' and 'Britain') and again in the final sentence through the collective noun 'phonies'. Even the seemingly less pejorative term 'migrant' in the headline suggests 'economic migrant', again to distinguish between this group and what the paper terms the 'genuine asylum seekers' who are in a clear minority. The piece therefore functions through a binary opposition – fake/genuine, dishonest/honest, majority/minority – which clearly agrees that migrants should be 'purged' from Britain. The implied violence of this verb, along with the more obvious antagonism in 'KOd' (meaning 'knocked out') and 'booted out', further encourages a combative, bigoted attitude which is typical of the xenophobic posturing towards 'foreigners' (whether they are resident abroad or in Britain) which is to be commonly found in the tabloids.

ACTIVITY 7:

Below is part of a report on the same story as it appeared in *The Guardian*, under a headline indicating that asylum-seekers were at liberty to remain in Britain. Read the piece through carefully and summarise the position which the journalist here is taking. How different is it from the position taken by the journalist in *The Sun*? Do you think *The Guardian*'s report is any more objective/balanced? What biases (if any) are evident? If you're working in a group, discuss your opinions with the other group members. When you have analysed the piece, write a couple of paragraphs comparing the approaches to the story taken by the different journalists.

> More than 30,000 asylum seekers and their families are to be allowed to stay in Britain under a limited amnesty unveiled by the Home Secretary, Jack Straw, yesterday in a one-off effort to cut the backlog of 76,000 cases.
>
> But this exemption is to be accompanied by a plan to disperse the remaining asylum seekers to approved hostels and bed and breakfast accommodation throughout Britain while their cases are heard.
>
> Applicants, who are banned from working, will not receive welfare benefits while their cases are decided. Instead they will mostly get help 'in kind' such as food vouchers. Cash payments will be kept to a minimum. 'What the genuine asylum seeker needs is food and shelter, not a Giro cheque,' Mr Straw said yesterday . . .
>
> Mr Straw said he hoped to clear the backlog and produce initial decisions on asylum cases within months by April 2001. A further £120 million is to be made available to clean up the system, officially described as a shambles.
>
> Ministers yesterday insisted that they were not declaring an amnesty for the 30,000 who have been waiting longer than 18 months for an official decision on their cases.
>
> (*The Guardian*, 28 July 1998: 2)

ACTIVITY 8:

The representation of asylum-seekers in the reports above is one example of the ways in which newspapers represent certain marginalised groups in British society. Using your selection of newspapers, examine how one other marginalised group is represented by the press. You might choose to examine, for example, the elderly, Muslims, homosexuals or the disabled. What kinds of language are used to refer to the groups of people you have chosen? Are there differences between the different newspapers? What does this tell you about the biases and/or ideological positions of the journalists?

We also need to consider two other methods by which journalists 'slant' their narratives – embedding and modality. *Embedding* refers to the way in which journalists incorporate a person's opinion into a news story in such a way as it appears to be a truth claim. For example, look at the paragraphs

below which are taken from an account of the deaths of Princess Diana and
Dodi Fayed in a car crash in Paris in 1997:

> The car which crashed killing Princess Diana and Dodi Fayed had faulty
> brakes, it was claimed yesterday.
>   Because they were 'unpredictable', the Mercedes 280S should not have
> been driven by someone who did not know its 'dangerous quirks', the car's
> usual driver said in a sworn statement to the French judge investigating
> the accident.
>
>   (*The Daily Mail*, 28 July 1998: 21)

Here, the whole story has its source in the testimony of one person. It is
therefore a matter of opinion, but it is embedded in the story in such a way
that the content of what is being said becomes more important than the
actual source. Look how the story starts, for example. The first sentence
opens with what seems to be definite objective truth – that the car in which
Diana and Dodi were travelling had defective brakes – and it is only at the
end of the sentence that we are informed that this is merely a claim. News
is often made out of such embedded texts and we need to be careful about
the way claims and facts are incorporated into any particular piece.

The concept of modality is also connected to the expression of claims
and facts, and relates specifically to the use of modal verbs. The modal verbs
are can/could, will/would, may/might, shall/should and must, and are used
to express degrees of *conviction*, *certainty* and *possibility*. For example, consider the following statements:

> Madonna will release a new album in the next few months.
> Madonna could release a new album in the next few months.
> Madonna may release a new album in the next few months.

The first of these statements is phrased as a fact – the album's release is
definitely going to happen. The second and third statements are both ways
of expressing the idea that the appearance of a new album is a possibility
but not definite. Some adverbs such as 'possibly', 'likely', 'probably' and
'certainly' can also be used in the same way. Journalists often manipulate
such words in order to suggest that an event is definitely going to happen,
when in reality it is impossible to know and a more cautious phrase should
be used. Speculation is not presented as such but rather assumes the status
of fact. In reading newspaper reports, therefore, it's very important to be
aware of the modal constructions being used.

The use of modal constructions is also an important issue in other types
of writing such as the academic essay, where making unsubstantiated or large
general claims is usually viewed as bad practice. For example, consider the

sentence 'D.H. Lawrence thought that sex was redemptive'. We might infer this from Lawrence's fiction, but as a factual statement it is too bold and sweeping. It would not carry much academic weight and therefore should be rephrased so that it is more specific. This can be achieved using the appropriate modal constructions: for example, 'From a close examination of parts of *Lady Chatterley's Lover*, it could be argued that Lawrence thought that sex was redemptive'. Similarly, the overly-bold statement 'Hardy was the last great novelist of the nineteenth century' certainly needs to be rewritten using a modal construction so that it is more cautious – perhaps being rephrased as 'It might be suggested that Hardy was the last great novelist of the nineteenth century'. In academic writing, it is imperative that the writer remains as objective as possible, an objectivity which, as we have seen, many journalists ignore or pretend to have when they really don't.

ACTIVITY 9:

Choose an article from one of your newspapers and identify where the writer uses embedding and modal verbs and phrases. Try to assess how much of the article is factual and how much of it is opinion or speculation. How easy is it to separate the two?

ACTIVITY 10:

You are a journalist for your local newspaper. Write a short news report (about 200 words) on a controversial event which has happened recently in your town/city. First write it as objectively as you can so that it is impossible to find any bias in it. Then rewrite it in order to give away bias very subtly by including up to ten key words which affect the tone.

ACTIVITY 11:

You are going to be interviewed for a job as a reporter on *The Guardian*. Buy a copy of *The Sun* one day this week. Choose an article that interests you and rewrite the article in the style of *The Guardian* which you can take to your interview to show that you understand and can employ the paper's house style. The article you choose should not be too long, and your own piece should be around 300 words. Alternatively, imagine that you are going for an interview at *The Sun* and rewrite an article of your choice from *The Guardian*.

Other types of journalism

Newspapers don't just report news, of course, and in the past ten years or so there has been an enormous expansion in the range of subjects covered in the papers. In the Sunday newspapers in particular, there has been a proliferation of supplements and stand-alone sections. *The Sunday Times*, for example, regularly contains separate sections on sport, money, travel, business, style, and culture, as well as the usual mixture of news, advertising and what is known as 'service information' – weather forecasts, TV programme listings, etc. Such a wide spectrum of interests and information means that many newspapers are often as long as an average novel and some even longer! Similarly, the last decade has seen an expanding trade in magazines. A visit to any large newsagent will reveal the huge number of consumer magazines, vocationally orientated magazines and specialist interest magazines available. *The Economist, Esquire, Farmer's Weekly, Gay Times, Marie Claire, Men's Health, National Geographic, New Scientist, New Statesman, Nursing Times, Q, Radio Times, Reader's Digest, TV Quick, Which?, Woman's Own* – the list is endless and, of course, the idea of writing in a suitable manner for a particular audience is crucial here, especially since many of these magazines are for specialised categories of readers.

In this final section of the chapter, we are going to explore some of the varieties of writing to be found in the extraordinarily diverse area of non-news journalism, although, of course, many of the ideas about structuring, language use and editing which we have examined in relation to writing news stories apply here as well. Let's start by thinking about feature articles, which make up the major part of most magazines and Sunday supplements. It is fair to argue that although the range of possible types of feature articles is huge, they usually differ from news story articles in two particular respects – their length and the time taken to write them. Typically, feature articles are longer than news story articles and they are generally written under less demanding time constraints, giving the writer more opportunity for research and reflection. Newspaper articles are usually required for the following day's paper (there isn't much point in reporting a news event two or more days after it has happened), whereas magazines and supplements might only appear once a week or once a month, therefore allowing deadlines to be more flexible.

Let's pause here for a moment to consider possible *sources* for articles. A news story will usually be based upon one or more of the following:

- an interview (with a person in the news or an eyewitness to a crash, for example)
- a press conference
- a press release from a public relations agency
- a government media briefing
- copy from an international news agency such as Reuter's or United Press International.

A feature article could also be based upon some of these, but is much more likely to be the result of the writer's extended reflection or investigation into a subject. For example, a feature writer might spend considerable time in a library in order to assess the importance of a contemporary writer or artist, or might undertake extensive testing of a range of new cars, wines or cosmetics. Alternatively, he or she may travel abroad to report on somewhere which might be of interest to a potential tourist, or be involved in a substantial amount of investigative interviewing.

Just as the range of possible subjects and approaches for feature articles is large, so is the range of styles in which such articles can be written. Very often, features contained within the same magazine or Sunday supplement are written by different people and so have very different styles. They might be written in a colloquial, chatty or confessional style, for example, or attempt to be more objective and authoritative. They could be spiced up with anecdotes or quotations from celebrities, or they might draw upon experts in a particular field to add weight to the piece. There is no end to the possible varieties.

ACTIVITY 12:

Below are excerpts from three feature articles published in very different magazines and supplements. The first deals with a visit to a country house. The second considers the impact of technology on everyday life. And the third reflects upon the work of the poet Carol Ann Duffy. Read them through carefully and then analyse their styles one by one. Use this exercise as an opportunity to consolidate the approaches and ideas which you have learnt during the course of this book. In your analysis you might like to consider the following: diction (is it complex or accessible? does the writer use any figures of speech?); register; tone; syntax and sentence structure; overall structure and development of argument; awareness of the audience. What do you think were the principal sources of information for each piece?

Extract 1

Hidden away down narrow high-hedgerowed lanes on the Somerset–Devon border, Cothay Manor is the sort of place that makes you wonder if, like Alice in Wonderland, you've sidestepped reality for the day. Divided into a series of 'rooms' by tall yew hedges – so thick you can't tell what's inside until you're halfway through the arch – there are little pocket-handkerchief lawns surrounded by borders of dreamy perfection, spilling a haze of colour and scent. From behind one hedge comes a mysterious splash from a swimming-pool that remains for ever undiscovered; through the arch of another a stone table, laid with a dish of pâté, three glasses and a bottle of wine, is visible. In the midday sun the only sound is the buzzing of the bees. And then, carrying over the hedges on the still air, comes a formidable female voice: 'If anyone wants to buy plants, I'm going to be here for ten more minutes only!' From out of nowhere, a dozen elderly ladies appear, clutching their handbags, and scurry off in the direction of the greenhouse.

(*The Sunday Telegraph*, 25 July 1999: 37)

Extract 2

Technology, eh? One minute it's making life easier, the next some lab rats come over all poorly. GM food, mobiles ... just how scared should we be?

You stagger in from work, unwrap some pre-packaged grub, throw it in the microwave and ring your mum on your mobile while you potter around waiting for dinner to cook. Which doesn't sound like a particularly death-defying scenario, does it? But according to some of the health scares doing the rounds, you could be taking your life in your hands.

For a start, has your dinner been genetically modified? And is the stuff it was wrapped in poisonous? What about the microwave – is it zapping you as well as your food? That mobile phone – frying your brain, is it ... ?

The shops are stuffed with things science has come up with to make modern life a doddle. Unfortunately, the minute something becomes indispensable, someone appears on the Nine O'Clock News declaring it dangerous. Before long, everyone's running round like headless chickens.

Genetically modified food is the latest, but by no means the only, health alert scaring us all out of our wits. So is all this technological time-saving killing us, or are we just a bunch of scaredy cats?

(*New Woman*, July 1999: 55)

Extract 3

In the world of British poetry, Carol Ann Duffy is a superstar. Highbrow and lowbrow, readers love her: from critics such as Sean O'Brien, who calls her 'the representative poet of her day', to students who study *Mean Time*, her majestic 1993 collection, as an A-level set text. Her poems are accessible and entertaining, yet her form is classical, her technique razor-sharp. She is read by people who don't really read poetry, yet she maintains the respect of her peers. Reviewers praise her touching, sensitive, witty evocations of love, loss, dislocation, nostalgia; fans talk of greeting her at readings 'with claps and cheers that would not sound out of place at a pop concert'. Here it is: she is easy, and she is good.

But her superstar status was noticed by the rest of the world only when the government decided not to make Duffy poet laureate after the death of Ted Hughes earlier this year – because, as a Downing Street official told a reporter, 'Blair is worried about having a homosexual as poet laureate because of how it might play in middle England.' Thus, Duffy became a caricature – the lesbian single-parent, with a black partner, from a Scottish working-class background – rejected in favour of Andrew Motion – similarly caricatured as a public-school, Oxford-educated, married, white male toff. The media set up an opposition between the Oxbridge-style poets who have the power: Motion, James Fenton, Craig Raine; and the 'postmodern provincials' who'd been rejected yet again: Duffy, Don Paterson, Liz Lochhead, Simon Armitage. The decision was labelled 'a disgrace', 'an insult to the country's intelligence' and, infamously, 'a bag o'shite'. Suddenly, Duffy was headline news, doorstepped by journalists obsessed with her sexuality, misquoted, a celebrity.

(*The Guardian Weekend*, 25 September 1999: 20)

ACTIVITY 13:

You're working as a freelance journalist and you've been asked by the editor of a local magazine in Manchester to write a short feature article (about 350 words) on the works of Elizabeth Gaskell. The magazine is circulated to all houses in the Greater Manchester area and so the piece must be suitable for a wide readership. Start by making a list of sources you might use to find appropriate information and then collect the material you need. Write a first draft and then edit and redraft it to produce a more polished version.

There are, of course, a whole range of genres other than the feature article which are included in magazines. One of these is the *review* – the synopsis of, and comment upon, a newly released or forthcoming book, CD, film, play or television programme. Here is an example taken from the music magazine *Q*:

Tori Amos: To Venus & Back

In 1992, after an earlier attempt at ridiculous rock chickery, Tori Amos decided to immerse herself in highbrow, singer-songwriter-style eccentricity; Kate Bush times infinity, if you will. The results worked wonders. Seven years and five albums on, Amos remains the perennial New Kook On the Block, with an often unhinged dramatic edge to her songs that some of her peers can only dream of emulating . . .

To Venus & Back is her most involving album to date. It's a rigorous listen, uneasy on the ears, and malevolently murky enough to suggest that Nine Inch Nails were loitering somewhere within the bowels of the studio . . .

(*Q*, November 1999: 116)

What's particularly interesting about this review is the way in which the writer has attempted to give a sense of Tori Amos's musical history and the impact of her new album through very vivid and playful language. Look at some of the phrases which are used – Amos is 'New Kook on the Block', an obvious pun on new kid on the block, and her songs have an 'unhinged' quality, suggesting the eccentricity of many of them. In the second paragraph here, there's an emphasis on a dark, almost demonic force working through the music – it is 'malevolently murky' and dark enough to suggest that the painful sounding group Nine Inch Nails were influencing it from the 'bowels' of the studio. This is a unique, and at times startling, way to review music, the idiosyncrasies of expression producing images and suggestions which are memorable and engaging. Compare this with the extract below taken from a review of the new edition of *The Oxford Book of English Verse*, which appeared in the *Times Literary Supplement* ('Q' here is a previous editor of the anthology):

> This hefty and handsome anthology appears almost a hundred years after Arthur Quiller-Couch's *Oxford Book of English Verse* (1900) – a widely loved work which sold half a million copies before 'Q' revised it in 1939, and which remains in print to this day, despite the rival publication of Helen Gardner's *New Oxford Book* in 1972. Whether Rick's innovative volume will be on sale a century from now depends on such imponderables as the future of English as a world language and the probable decline of print in the face of electronic technology, but his publishers have spared no effort in giving his book a good start in life. Stoutly bound in blue and gold, and wrapped in a parchment-thick jacket adorned with quill pens, the facsimile of a Shakespeare sonnet, and what looks like National Trust wallpaper, this is scholarship as heritage object, marketed with one eye on the academy but the other on mail-order book clubs.
>
> (*Times Literary Supplement*, 15 October 1999: 27)

This is the opening paragraph of a long review on the new anthology but is representative of the whole in being a lot more reserved and less playful than the review of the new Tori Amos album. It is a very factual account with a rather sombre tone, despite the satirical jibe at the marketing of the text as 'heritage object'. In its place, however, this review is no less effective than the more light-hearted music review. As we have emphasised throughout, it is all a matter of audience. The writers of these different reviews expect to be addressing very different readers and therefore adapt their language and style accordingly.

ACTIVITY 14:

From your magazines, collect examples of two or three reviews of books, music, films or television programmes, and write a short paragraph describing the differences in style between them. Then write your own review of a book you have recently read, a CD you have bought or a film/TV programme you have seen, imitating the style of one of the published reviews.

ACTIVITY 15:

Two other very popular genres within magazines are the problem page and the horoscope. Choose one of these and collect a range of published examples. Make a list of the key elements contained in the genre and then write your own. You might like to write a parody of the examples you have collected (check Chapter 2 for more information on parody). Add a short paragraph reflecting on what you have written.

Summary

In this chapter we have examined and/or revised:

- the importance of being aware of the audience for which you are writing
- the language and construction of headlines
- the structure and style of articles
- the importance of editing
- the biases embedded in writing
- a range of journalistic genres.

Reference

Waterhouse, Keith (1993) *Waterhouse on Newspaper Style*. London: Penguin.

GLOSSARY

Tory Young

alliteration   Repetition of initial consonants or consonant clusters (e.g. the hissing, slithering snake).

assonance   Recurrent use of the same or similar vowels to achieve a specific effect.

collocation   Two or more words which are commonly found together (e.g. *blinding flash* or *uphill struggle*).

colloquial phrases   Language used in conversation or informal, familiar contexts.

conjunctions   Words that connect other words or phrases (e.g. day *and* night); classified into co-ordinating (e.g. *and*) and subordinating (e.g. *until*).

copy   A term used in journalism to describe the article or text a journalist submits to a paper or magazine.

denotation   What appears to be the core meaning of a word, as distinct from its cultural connotations or personal associations. For instance, whilst *alcoholic beverage*, *pint*, *drink* and *tipple* all have similar denotations, their connotations are different.

diction   Choice of words, especially the vocabulary used by a poet or writer.

discourse   (i) A particular conversation or dialogue in general; (ii) text longer than a sentence; (iii) communicative practices expressing the interests of a particular socio-historical group or institution.

discourse worlds/ discourse communities   Types of specialist language spoken by a particular group of people in a particular context: for instance the language of nurses or newspaper journalists.

embedding   Inserting one grammatical unit within another, often used in journalism (e.g. '*The Queen is very unhappy about the situation*', a close source revealed).

emotive words   Words used to arouse particular emotions.

field   A loose term used to describe words which are commonly associated with reference to a particular topic; for instance, *steam, sauté, olive oil, frying pan* and *bake* could all be said to belong to a field called *cooking*.

genre   Categories of literature (e.g. poetry, novel, drama), which can be broken down into sub-genres (e.g. comedies and tragedies in drama). These categories relate to form, content and function, and may overlap.

homonym   A word with the same spelling or pronunciation as another, but with a different meaning or origin (e.g. take the first turning on your *right* / you know I am always *right*).

homophones   Words which sound the same but which have a different meaning or spelling (e.g. *knight/night, there/their*).

hyperbole   Emphatic exaggeration (e.g. *I've told you a thousand times*).

idioms   Phrases with meanings which are not easily determined from the constituent parts (e.g. *get the sack* or *visit the ladies*).

jargon   Another phrase for the specialised language of discourse worlds, but is often used pejoratively to mean the excessive use of overspecialised words.

lexicon/lexis   The vocabulary of a language, especially in dictionary form.

malapropism   An inappropriate word, mistakenly used because it sounds like the intended word (e.g. *suggestive* biscuits instead of *digestive* biscuits).

metaphor   Talking of one thing in terms of another (e.g. *Your room is a pigsty*).

modality   Features of language which express the speaker's opinions or perspectives (e.g. I *really wouldn't* do that if I were you).

mode   The medium of communication (e.g. letter, e-mail, answerphone message).

modifiers (pre-modifiers, post-modifiers)   Words in a noun phrase before or after the head noun which are grammatically dependent on it and alter or modify its meaning. For instance, in the noun phrase '*that chic little* skirt *in the window*', the pre-modifiers and post-modifiers have been italicised.

neologism   The creation of a new word out of existing elements (e.g. *tabloidese* below).

nominalisation   The name given to a noun when it is formed from a verb (e.g. *reproduction* from the verb *to reproduce*).

noun phrases   A grammatical item of more than one word organised around a noun. In the following sentence the whole noun phrase has been italicised: 'I'm going to buy *those silver jeans in the window*'.

open/closed class words   Nouns, adjectives, adverbs and verbs are called open word classes because they are evolving and expanding in number as language changes with society. Pronouns, conjunctions, determiners and prepositions generally do not change or increase in number.

parody   A deliberately exaggerated imitation of a style, genre or writer, often written to humorous effect and sometimes with affection.

pastiche   An imitation of a particular style or writer.

purple prose   Writing which is considered too elaborate, containing many adjectives and adverbs.

register   The variety of language used, relating to purpose and situation.

semantics   The study of linguistic meanings.

skaz   Written language which sounds more like thought or speech.

synonyms   A word that has the same meaning, in a particular context, as another word.

syntax   The order and structure of words and clauses in a sentence.

tabloidese   A style of language used and developed in tabloid journalism.

tautology   An unnecessary repetition of a word or idea (e.g. We've had an *annual* conference *every year*).

tenor   The speaker/writer's relationship with the recipient of the talk/ writing which informs register and diction.

FURTHER READING

Bacon, Francis (1985) *The Essays*, ed. John Pitcher. Harmondsworth: Penguin.
Bell, Alan (1991) *The Language of News Media*. Oxford: Basil Blackwell.
Bex, T. (1996) *Variety in Written English: Texts in Society/Societies in Text*. London: Routledge.
Bowring, M., Carter, R., Goddard, A., Reah, D. and Sanger, K. (1997) *Working with Texts: A Core Book for Language Analysis*. London: Routledge.
Briggs, Adam and Cobley, Paul (eds) (1998) *The Media: An Introduction*. London: Longman.
Carter, Ron and Nash, Walter (1990) *Seeing Through Language: A Guide to Styles of English Writing*. Oxford: Blackwell.
Crystal, David and Davie, Donald (1969) *Investigating English Style*. London: Longman.
Cutts, Martin (1995) *The Plain English Guide*. Oxford: Oxford University Press.
Davies Roberts, Philip (1987) *Plain English: A User's Guide*. Harmondsworth: Penguin.
Davis, Anthony (1988) *Magazine Journalism Today*. Oxford: Heinemann.
Dolon, John (1996) *Writing Well, Speaking Clearly*. Dunedin, New Zealand: University of Otago Press.
Fabb, Nigel and Durant, Alan (1993) *How to Write Essays, Dissertations and Theses for Literary Studies*, London: Longman.
Fowler, Roger (1991) *Language in the News: Discourse and Ideology in the Press*. London: Routledge.
Goatley, Andrew (1999) *Critical Reading and Writing: Discovering Ideology in Discourse*. London: Routledge.
Graham, Betsey P. (1980) *Magazine Article Writing: Substance and Style*. New York: Holt, Rinehart and Winston.
Halliday, M.A.K. and Hasan, R. (1989) *Language, Context and Text: Aspects of Language in a Social-Semiotic Perspective*. Oxford: Oxford University Press.
Harris, Joseph (1994) *Style: Ten Lessons in Grace and Clarity*. London: HarperCollins.
Hartley, John (1982) *Understanding News*. London: Routledge.
Hines, John (1987) *The Way to Write Magazine Articles*. London: Elm Tree Books.
Hope, J. and Wright, L. (1996) *Stylistics: A Practical Coursebook*. London: Routledge.
Leech, Geoffrey and Short, Mick (1981) *Style in Fiction*. London: Longman.

Nash, Walter and Stacey, David (1997) *Creating Texts: An Introduction to the Study of Composition*. London: Longman.

Plain English Campaign (1996) *Language on Trial: The Plain English Guide to Legal Writing*. London: Robson Books Ltd.

Reah, Danuta (1998) *The Language of Newspapers*. London: Routledge.

Ross, Alison (1998) *The Language of Humour*. London: Routledge.

Short, Mick (1996) *Exploring Language in Poems, Prose and Plays*. London: Longman.

Waterhouse, Keith (1993) *Waterhouse on Newspaper Style*. London: Penguin.

Williams, Joseph M. (1989) *Style*. Glenview, Illinois: Scott, Foresman and Co.

INDEX